OK 2

TOTALLY TRUE

Building Vocabulary Through Reading

OXFORD

UNIVERSITY PRESS

OXFORD
UNIVERSITY PRESS

198 Madison Avenue
New York, NY 10016 USA

Great Clarendon Street, Oxford OX2 6DP UK

Oxford University Press is a department of the University of Oxford.
It furthers the University's objective of excellence in research, scholarship,
and education by publishing worldwide in

Oxford New York

Auckland Cape Town Dar es Salaam Hong Kong Karachi
Kuala Lumpur Madrid Melbourne Mexico City Nairobi
New Delhi Shanghai Taipei Toronto

With offices in

Argentina Austria Brazil Chile Czech Republic France Greece
Guatemala Hungary Italy Japan Poland Portugal Singapore
South Korea Switzerland Thailand Turkey Ukraine Vietnam

OXFORD and OXFORD ENGLISH are registered trademarks of
Oxford University Press.

© Oxford University Press 2005

Database right Oxford University Press (maker)

Library of Congress Cataloging-in-Publication Data

Huizenga, Jann.
   Totally true : building vocabulary through reading. Book 2 / Jann Huizenga.
   p. cm.
   Includes index.
   ISBN-13: 978-0-19-430204-3
   ISBN-10: 0-19-430204-0
    1. Vocabulary—Problems, exercises, etc. 2. English language—
Textbooks for foreign speakers. I. Title.

PE1449.H825 2005
428.6'4-dc22

2004065422

Executive Publisher: Nancy Leonhardt
Senior Acquisitions Editor: Chris Balderston
Editor: Emma Gonin
Assistant Editor: Hannah Ryu
Assistant Editor: Kate Schubert
Art Director: Maj-Britt Hagsted
Design Project Manager: Amelia Carling
Senior Designer: Michael Steinhofer
Layout Artist: Julie Macus
Senior Art Editor: Jodi Waxman
Production Manager: Shanta Persaud
Production Controller: Eve Wong

ISBN-13: 978 0 19 430204 3
ISBN-10: 0 19 430204 0

Printed in China.

10 9 8 7 6 5 4 3 2

ACKNOWLEDGMENTS

Cover photographs: Sunset: © Fogstock/Alamy; Skydiver: © Buzz Pictures/Alamy;
Surfer: © Buzz Pictures/Alamy; Taipei 101: © Associated Press.

Illustrations by: Adrian Barclay pp. 11, 19, 31, 39, 44, 51, 63, 71, 79; Jun Park pp. 8,
16, 20, 24, 32, 54 (Match the words), 68, 76; George Thompson pp. 23, 35, 40, 43,
54 (barbecue), 60, 64, 80, 82 (cafe); Joe VanDerBos pp. 4, 26 (Match the words), 48,
52, 82 (Match the words); William Waitzman pp. 3, 7, 12, 15, 26 (park), 36, 47,
59, 67, 72, 75.

We would like to thank the following for their permission to reproduce photographs:
A.B./H. Winkler/Masterfile p.84; AGE Fotostock p. 51; Agence France Press/Getty
Images p.13; Ed Alcock p.22; Arena Images p.53; Associated Press pp. 46, 50, 58,
62, 70; Bettmann/Corbis p. 81; Brand X Pictures/Alamy pp. 10, 21; Buzz
Pictures/Alamy p.49; Digital Vision/Getty Images pp. 14, 69; Fotosonline/Alamy
p.6; Stephen Frink Collection/Alamy p. 65; Earl Harper/Ecostock p. 18; Susan
Hreljac p.77; Jann Huizenga p.17; Imagesource/Alamy p.5; Peter LaMastro/Getty
Images p.9; Kansas City Star p.38; Photodisc p. 42; The Photolibrary Wales/Alamy
p.56; Andrea Pistolesi/Getty Images p.73; Reuters/Pawel Kopczynski p. 74;
Reuters/Brian Snyder p.28; Lynn Richards p.37; Ted Soqui/Corbis p.78; Charles
Thatcher/Getty Images p.25; Chris Theren/The Augusta Chronicle p.66;
Thinkstock/Alamy p.2; Ting-Li Wang/The New York Times p.41; Maximilian
Weinzierl/Alamy p.45, Yellow Dog Productions/Getty Images, p.34.

Special thanks to: The World Kindness Movement, p. 30.

Unit Tests (available online) written by: Andy London

Contents

To the Student iv

A Letter to Teachers vi

Totally *Bookworms* Compatible vii

Teaching Suggestions viii

Acknowledgments xi

1 Trouble at the Airport 2

2 Smart Guard 6

3 School Clothes 10

4 It's Hard to Stop! 14

5 Stuck in the Mud 18

6 Cops on Wheels 22

   Review: Units 1–6 26

7 Try a Little Kindness 30

8 Girls Save Falling Child 34

9 The Wedding Dress 38

10 A Worm a Day 42

11 Miracle Woman 46

12 Boy Genius 50

   Review: Units 7–12 54

13 Fighting Crime with Books 58

14 Back in the Water Again 62

15 Cows Prefer Beethoven 66

16 A Cool Hotel 70

17 Small Woman Is Big Hero 74

18 The Smartest Home 78

   Review: Units 13–18 82

   Dictations 86

   Glossary 88

   Index 97

Welcome to *Totally True*. Let's take a look at a unit.

1. Read the story asks you to predict what the story is about, read it, and get to know the New Words.

2. Rate the story asks about your interest in the story.

3. Check your comprehension asks how well you understand the story.

4. Check your vocabulary helps you practice the New Words by completing sentences about the story.

5. Listen to the story gives you the chance to hear the story as you look at the pictures.

6. Retell the story helps you practice retelling the story using the pictures.

1
Trouble at the Airport

1. Read the story
Look at the pictures on these pages. What is the story about? Now read it.

REGINA, CANADA ¹A woman was at an airport in Canada, in a hurry to catch her plane. When she went through the **metal detector***, it made a noise. *Bzzz!* ²Airport **officials** carefully **checked** her. There were no **coins** in her pockets and no metal in her shoes. ³They told her to walk through again. *Bzzz!* The officials **searched** her once again. There was nothing! ⁴Finally, they **let** her **pass** and **board** the plane.
⁵**Several** days later, the woman had a **stomachache**. She went to her doctor and got an X-ray**. There was a 30-centimeter-long metal **instrument** in her stomach from an old **operation**. She was **surprised** and angry. So that was why she had a stomachache—and all the trouble at the airport!
⁶"Everyone makes mistakes," a hospital official explained. "No one is **perfect**."

* detector: something that finds metal
** X-ray: a photo of the inside of your body

NEW WORDS

metal *n*	check *v*	search *v*	pass *v*	several *adj*	instrument *n* surprised *adj*
official *n*	coin *n*	let *v*	board *v*	stomachache *n*	operation *n* perfect *adj*

>> See Glossary on page 88. >>

2. Rate the story
How much did you like it? Mark an ✗.

Not at All ① ② ③ ④ ⑤ A Lot

2   Unit 1

3. Check your comprehension
Put the sentences in the correct order. Number them 1–7. The first one is done for you.
a. ___ Airport officials checked her.
b. ___ Now the woman understood her trouble at the airport!
c. ___ Later, the woman got an X-ray because she had a stomachache.
d. ___ The airport officials finally let her get on the plane.
e. ___ The doctor found a long metal instrument in her stomach.
f. _1_ The woman walked through the metal detector, and it made a noise.
g. ___ They found no coins or metal.

4. Check your vocabulary
Complete the sentences with the New Words.
a. Airport officials s_ _ _ched the woman, but she had no c_ _ _ _ in her pockets.
b. They finally let her p_ _ _ and bo_ _ _ the plane.
c. Sev_ _ _ _ days later, the woman's doctor found a metal instr_ _ _ _ _ in her stomach.
d. A hospital off_ _ _ _ _ later explained that no one is pe_ _ _ _ _.

5. Listen to the story track 2
Now listen to the story two or three times. Look at the pictures below as you listen.

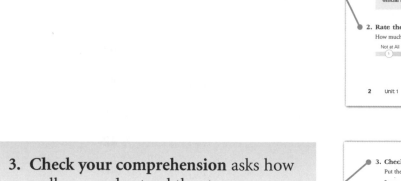

6. Retell the story
Cover the story and look at the pictures above. Retell the story using the New Words.

Unit 1   3

7. Answer the questions asks you to talk about the story and yourself.

8. Learn word partnerships builds on what you have learned by introducing words that go with one or two of the New Words.

9. Learn word groups builds on what you have learned by using pictures to introduce more vocabulary related to the New Words.

---

7. Answer the questions

About the story...
a. Why did airport officials search the woman?
b. Why did she go to her doctor?
c. How did she feel after the X-ray?
d. How do you think the mistake at the hospital happened?

About you...
e. Do you like airports? Why or why not?
f. Have you ever had trouble at an airport? What happened?
g. What do you do when you get a stomachache?
h. Have you ever had an operation? How did you feel?

8. Learn word partnerships

Study the partnerships below. Complete the sentences so they are true for you.

LET	
let someone do something	***Airport officials let the woman board the plane.*** *My teacher lets us drink tea in class.* *I let my friend Eun-mi use my bike.* *My sister doesn't let me listen to her CDs.*

a. My English teacher lets students _____
b. He/she doesn't let _____
c. I let my friend _____

9. Learn word groups

Complete the sentences so they are true for you. Use words from the pictures.

FEELING SICK

a stomachache   a headache   a cough   a cut   a bruise   a broken leg

a. When I have _____, I drink tea or water.
b. I have never had _____
c. I had _____ last year.

4   Unit 1

---

10. Take a dictation gives you practice listening to a summary of the story and writing down what you hear.

11. Complete the story gives you a second story to review the New Words and other new vocabulary.

Talk about the stories gives you the chance to talk more about both stories.

---

10. Take a dictation track 3
Use your own paper to write the dictation. Check your answers on page 86.

11. Complete the story
Use the words from the box to complete the story.

| let | cough | official | surprised |
| several | metal | checked | operation |

A Strange Cough

TAIPEI, TAIWAN   For many years, a Taiwanese man had a bad **(1)** _____ Finally, he went to see his doctor. The doctor **(2)** _____ him carefully but did not find anything wrong. **(3)** "_____ me take an X-ray," the doctor said.

The X-ray showed a piece of **(4)** _____ deep in the man's back. It was a large needle*, and it was near the man's lungs**. The man was **(5)** _____. How did the needle get there? When he told his wife about it, she looked surprised, too. "Oh, dear!" she said. "I remember now. I lost a needle on our bed **(6)** _____ years ago!"

A hospital **(7)** _____ said that the needle was dangerously close to the man's lungs. He had an **(8)** _____ and now the needle and the man's cough are gone.

*needle: a small piece of metal with a hole that you use to make clothes
**lungs: two parts inside your body that you use to breathe

Talk about the stories
How are the stories of the Canadian woman and the Taiwanese man similar? How are they different?

Unit 1   5

v

Dear Teachers,

Welcome to *Totally True*! If you are looking for an enjoyable and motivating way to help build your students' vocabulary, you've come to the right place. Vocabulary learning doesn't have to be difficult and dull. The goal of *Totally True* Book 2 is to make it fun. It teaches common words in the context of amazing true stories at a high-beginner level. The book is intended for classroom use, but it will also work well for self-study with the audio CD.

Totally True was written with two things in mind: 1) that everyone loves a great story and 2) that students acquire new vocabulary more readily when they meet it in engaging contexts and then use it in purposeful follow-up activities.

Research on vocabulary acquisition shows that most learning takes place when students meet new words in context, not in isolation. The content must be rich and interesting, and—even more importantly—understandable. The stories in *Totally True* satisfy these conditions: they are intrinsically entertaining while the accompanying pictures make them easy to understand.

The research suggests that context alone, however, is not enough for many students to learn new vocabulary. Formal, explicit instruction can help. Thus *Totally True* highlights new vocabulary in the opening stories and helps students to focus on this vocabulary in varied activities throughout the rest of each unit.

How can we make sure that new vocabulary will remain in students' long-term memories? At least two things are necessary: First, students need to process the vocabulary at a deep level—that is, they need to produce it. *Totally True* provides many opportunities for students to use the new vocabulary items in both speaking and writing, in meaningful and personalized ways. Second, students need multiple meaningful exposures to the vocabulary (as many as 7–12 times, some experts say). *Totally True* provides careful recycling—students revisit each new vocabulary item several times within each unit, as well as in the review units, and to some extent from unit to unit. The index on pages 97–99 shows where the vocabulary items are recycled. *Totally True* thoroughly integrates the four strands of listening, reading, speaking, and writing, and its activities are sequenced so that work on receptive skills precedes production. The book can be successfully used for general language acquisition or reading instruction as well as for the specific mastery of vocabulary.

I encourage you to adapt the material to suit the needs of your classes. I really hope you enjoy using the book, and I wish you every success.

Jann Huizenga

Totally *Bookworms* Compatible

A key benefit of *Totally True* is that its language levels are tied to the *Oxford Bookworms* syllabus, so the series can be used together with *Bookworms* graded readers. The stories in *Totally True* Book 2 use the core structures and the vocabulary from *Bookworms* Stage 2. However, each opening story introduces 10–14 words above Stage 2. These words are highlighted in the story and treated as "New Words." Meeting these higher-level New Words initially in the rich context of a story helps students to understand them. Students continue to meet and produce the New Words in the activities throughout the unit, ensuring that these words become part of students' active vocabulary. Studying with *Totally True* Book 2 will help prepare students to move up to *Bookworms* Stage 3. *Totally True* can also complement any other extensive reading program. The stories and carefully designed practice activities will provide variety in teaching reading.

Level	Vocabulary	Core structures include:	Examples from *Totally True*
Oxford Bookworms Stage 1 and *Totally True* Book 1	400 headwords	simple present present continuous simple past	The boy does not like to be away from his **favorite** friend. Once the family took a **trip**, but they did not stay away long. "My son **missed** Lucky," said his mother. "So we came back early." *Python Boy* (Unit 2)
Oxford Bookworms Stage 2 and *Totally True* Book 2	700 headwords	present perfect *will* (future) *have to / must not could*	The city has given free books to subway riders **since** 2004, and wants to **give away** millions more in the future. The city hopes that readers will **return** the books when they finish, but no one is checking. *Fighting Crime with Books* (Unit 13)
Oxford Bookworms Stage 3 and *Totally True* Book 3	1,000 headwords	present perfect continuous past perfect *used to*	**Meanwhile**, their dinner was still cooking on the **stove** in the kitchen. They had completely forgotten about it! It started to burn, and the **flames** jumped quickly around the kitchen. The whole room and a nearby hallway were completely destroyed. *Cat and Couple Are Homeless* (Unit 13)

Teaching Suggestions

1. Read the story

Purpose: To engage students' attention, to train them to use prediction as a pre-reading strategy, to develop general reading comprehension skills, and to introduce the New Words in context.

Procedure: Before students read, ask them to cover the story and look at the pictures on the opposite page. As students make predictions about the story, help them with the vocabulary they need—especially key words and New Words from the story. If students call out words or phrases in their native language, translate them into English and write them on the board. Then ask students to read the story silently to see if their predictions are correct. Tell them to make their best guess about the meanings of the New Words—the words in bold. Tell students the numbered sentences in the story correspond to the numbered pictures. Within the context of the story and with the support of the pictures, students should be able to make good guesses.

After the first reading, students can check the meanings of the New Words in the glossary on pages 88–96. Encourage them to read the story again after this.

Alternative procedure: After students look at the pictures, ask them to write two or three questions they have about the story. Ask them to read the story to see if they can find answers to their questions.

2. Rate the story

Purpose: To encourage students to respond personally to the story and to develop critical reading and thinking skills, such as evaluating and giving opinions.

Procedure: After students mark an **✗** on the scale, ask them to share the reasons for their ratings with a partner or a small group.

Instead of having students do the "Rate the story" activity here, you could have them do it after activity 7. Alternatively, they could rate the story here and again after activity 7 to see if their opinions have changed.

Alternative procedure: If you have a small class, hang five pieces of paper in different places on the wall of your classroom. Each paper shows a different number from 1 to 5. After students have marked an **✗** on the scale, ask them to stand up and walk to the number that shows how they rated the story. Ask them to speak to one member of their group to explain their opinion of the story. After a minute, ask a few volunteers to share what they heard with the whole class.

3. Check your comprehension

Purpose: To see how well students understand the general meaning of the story.

Procedure: Encourage students to complete this activity without looking back at the story. Then have students compare their answers with a partner or a small group. If the activity causes difficulty, have students read the story a second time and try the activity again.

4. Check your vocabulary

Purpose: To help students focus on the use and spelling of the New Words, a first step in making the New Words part of their active vocabulary.

Procedure: Encourage students to complete this activity without looking back at the story. Then have students check their answers against the story or compare them with a partner or small group.

Alternative procedure: If the activity causes difficulty, have students complete it while looking at the story.

5. Listen to the story

Purpose: To give students an opportunity to hear the story and the New Words, and to prepare them to retell the story.

Procedure: Ask students to look only at the numbered pictures (not at the story). Play the CD. Students will probably want to hear the story more than once. Afterward, to assess students' listening, read the story to students yourself, making some factual "mistakes." Tell students to clap when they hear a mistake and then see if anyone in the class can correct it.

If you don't have the CD, read the story to students yourself. Say the numbers as you read so that students can look at the relevant picture at the right time.

Alternative procedure: To reinforce the New Words, write them on the board and point to them as the CD is playing. This will be especially appreciated by your more visually-oriented students.

6. Retell the story

Purpose: To give students oral practice, with a combined focus on story retelling and additional practice of the New Words.

Procedure: Have students cover the story and look only at the pictures. Elicit the story orally from the whole class first. Encourage students to call out the ideas of the story in chronological order and to use the New Words, telling them to paraphrase. Then ask students to practice retelling the story in their own words with a partner.

Alternative procedure: Put students in small groups and have them retell the entire story together by taking turns contributing a sentence at a time.

7. Answer the questions

Purpose: To encourage students to discuss the story, to relate it to their personal lives, and to meet and use the New Words in meaningful and personalized contexts.

Procedure: Ask students one of the questions from this activity. Give them time to think about the answer and then have them discuss it with a partner or a small group. Ask a volunteer or two to report back to the whole class. Then ask another question.

Alternative procedure for "About the story": To make sure all your students are involved in this activity simultaneously, follow this procedure:

a. Put students in small groups. Four is the ideal number.
b. Give each student a number (from 1 to 4).
c. Ask one of the "About the story" questions.
d. Tell students to decide on the answer together in their groups.
e. After about a minute, call a number (1, 2, 3, or 4). Have students with that number stand up and report back on their group's answer.

Alternative procedure for "About you": To provide students with some writing practice, allow each student to choose the one question that most interests him/her. Give students a time limit of about five minutes to write their answers. Then have students share their answers with a small group.

8. Learn word partnerships

Purpose: To build on what students have learned by introducing key collocations for one or two of the New Words.

Procedure: Tell students that they are going to learn a little more about one or two of the New Words. Have students study the chart. Explain that the New Word(s) in black often occur(s) with the words in orange. Tell students that when they meet any new vocabulary, they should look at the words that surround it because learning a new word together with its "word partners" will lead to fluency faster than learning a word in isolation. This technique will also make them more accurate users of the language. Have students complete the sentences individually, and then ask them to share their answers with a partner or a small group.

9. Learn word groups

Purpose: To build on what students have learned by introducing new vocabulary that is thematically related to one or more of the New Words.

Procedure: Students already know one or two of the New Words pictured here, but they may not know the other words that are thematically related to it/them. Pronounce the words and allow students to repeat them. Then have students complete the sentences and share their answers with a partner or a small group.

10. Take a dictation

Purpose: To assess if students can hear and write the New Words in a story summary.

Procedure: Play the dictation on the CD and ask students to write what they hear—there is a pause after each breath group so they have time to write.

Play the dictation again to allow students to check their answers. Students then correct their work or their partner's work by looking at pages 86–87. You could use this as a test and collect the dictations.
Alternative procedure: Read the dictation yourself at normal speed. Students should not write at this stage. Then read it again, pausing after each breath group so that students have time to write. Read the dictation a third time, at near-normal speed, allowing students to check their answers. Students then correct their work or their partner's work by looking at pages 86–87. Again, you could use this as a test and collect the dictations.

11. Complete the story

Purpose: To give students an opportunity to review the New Words, and other vocabulary from the unit, in a new context, and to provide additional reading practice using a story that is thematically related to the first one.
Procedure: Encourage students to complete this story individually, and then have them check their answers with a partner or a small group. They could then practice reading the story to each other.
Alternative procedure: If you have more advanced students, have them cover the story and try to retell it in their own words, using the words in the box.

Talk about the stories

Purpose: To give students additional oral practice using the New Words in a less structured way, and to develop critical thinking skills such as evaluating, comparing, contrasting, and giving opinions.
Procedure: There are two types of "Talk about the stories": discussion questions and role plays. For the discussion questions, give students a bit of thinking time. Then have them discuss their ideas with a small group or you could conduct a whole-class discussion.

For the role plays, have students work with a partner. Give them a time limit of a few minutes for their "conversation." You may have brave volunteers who want to reenact their conversation for the whole class!

Web Searches

If your students want additional information about a story, have them do a Web search by inserting a name or a topic into a search engine. This could be done as classwork or homework. At the time of publication, most of the stories could be found on the Internet.

Audio CD

The CD contains recordings of the first stories in each unit and the dictations. These are read by native speakers and provide great listening models and variety in class. You may prefer to play the story for students in activity 1, changing the focus of the activity from reading comprehension to pronunciation.

Totally True Teacher's Resource Site

The Teacher's Resource Site has downloadable Unit Tests that review all the New Words from each unit and help teachers and students assess progress. Answer Keys for these tests and for *Totally True* Book 2 are also available at www.oup.com/elt/teacher/totallytrue.

Acknowledgments

I would like to thank those folks who helped me find the great stories for this book—my generous and talented colleagues Won-Mi Jeong and Stella Chen, my brother Joel (with his piles of clippings), and my stalwart husband Kim (who spent countless hours finding and critiquing stories and then figuring out how to illustrate them). Thanks also to my father, John, who never complained when his tidy kitchen was transformed into my temporary office during visits.

I am also grateful to all the teachers and students in Asia who have participated in my recent workshops. Their creative ideas and enthusiasm helped shape this series. These people include the brilliant and hospitable teachers and students at De Lin Institute of Technology in Taipei—in particular Fanny Lai, Stella Chen, Felisa Li, Gloria Chen, and Shi-tung Chuang; the unforgettable teachers from the Korean National University of Education—especially Won-Mi Jeong, Eun-Jeong Ji, Young-Chai Son, Hee-Jung Park, Sun-Mi Kim, Jin-a Choe, Young-Hee Moon, Hyo-Gyoung Lim, and Joo-In Chang; and all the dear colleagues from Kumamoto Prefecture in Japan—including Rika Muraoka, Naomi Osada, Masaya Shindate, Hideaki Kiya, and Yayoi Umeda. It was an honor to work with everyone.

I'd like to give a special, heartfelt thanks to Dorota Holownia and Candy Veas, whose creativity and high spirits, as well as their intellectual and moral support on this and other projects, are always treasured.

Colleagues and students in Sicily, where much of this book was written, have also played an important role in this work, and I thank them for their very special friendships: Anna Reitano, Mary Puccia, Simona Barone, Giovanna Battaglia, Davide Fiorito, Simona Gambino, Antonella Gulino, Francesca Flaccavento, Rosaria Leone, and Giovanna Vernuccio.

In addition, I'd like to thank the following OUP staff for their support and assistance in the development of *Totally True*: Janet Aitchison, Oliver Bayley, Nick Bullard, Julia Chang, Tina Chen, Steven Ferguson, Satoko Fukazawa, JJ Lee, Constance Mo, Paul Riley, Amany Sarkiz, Julie Till, and Ted Yoshioka.

Finally, the publisher and the author would like to thank the following teachers whose comments, reviews, and assistance were instrumental in the development of *Totally True*: Young-sung Chueh, Kumiko Fushino, Paul Jen, Sue Kim, Yonghyun Kwon, Richard S. Lavin, Jong-Chul Seo, James Sims, Daniel Stewart, Ching-Yi Tien, Carol Vaughan, Lisa D. Vogt, Gerald Williams, and Mei-ling Wu.

1

Trouble at the Airport

1. Read the story

Look at the pictures on these pages.
What is the story about? Now read it.

REGINA, CANADA **¹**A woman was at an airport in Canada, in a hurry to catch her plane. When she went through the **metal** detector*, it made a noise. *Bzzz!* **²**Airport **officials** carefully **checked** her. There were no **coins** in her pockets and no metal in her shoes. **³**They told her to walk through again. *Bzzz!* The officials **searched** her once again. There was nothing! **⁴**Finally, they **let** her **pass** and **board** the plane.

⁵Several days later, the woman had a **stomachache**. She went to her doctor and got an X-ray**. There was a 30-centimeter-long metal **instrument** in her stomach from an old **operation**. She was **surprised** and angry. So that was why she had a stomachache—and all the trouble at the airport!

⁶"Everyone makes mistakes," a hospital official explained. "No one is **perfect**."

---

* detector: something that finds metal
** X-ray: a photo of the inside of your body

NEW WORDS

metal *n*	check *v*	search *v*	pass *v*	several *adj*	instrument *n*	surprised *adj*
official *n*	coin *n*	let *v*	board *v*	stomachache *n*	operation *n*	perfect *adj*

>> See Glossary on page 88. >>

2. Rate the story

How much did you like it? Mark an ✗.

Not at All   A Lot

  ①   ②   ③   ④   ⑤

3. Check your comprehension

Put the sentences in the correct order. Number them 1–7. The first one is done for you.

a. ___ Airport officials checked her.

b. ___ Now the woman understood her trouble at the airport!

c. ___ Later, the woman got an X-ray because she had a stomachache.

d. ___ The airport officials finally let her get on the plane.

e. ___ The doctor found a long metal instrument in her stomach.

f. _1_ The woman walked through the metal detector, and it made a noise.

g. ___ They found no coins or metal.

4. Check your vocabulary

Complete the sentences with the New Words.

a. Airport officials s_ _ _ched the woman, but she had no c_ _ _ _ in her pockets.

b. They finally let her p_ _ _ and bo_ _ _ the plane.

c. Sev_ _ _ _ days later, the woman's doctor found a metal instr_ _ _ _ _ in her stomach.

d. A hospital off_ _ _ _ _ later explained that no one is pe_ _ _ _ _.

5. Listen to the story track 2

Now listen to the story two or three times. Look at the pictures below as you listen.

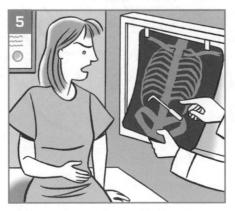

6. Retell the story

Cover the story and look at the pictures above. Retell the story using the New Words.

7. Answer the questions

About the story…
a. Why did airport officials search the woman?
b. Why did she go to her doctor?
c. How did she feel after the X-ray?
d. How do you think the mistake at the hospital happened?

About you…
e. Do you like airports? Why or why not?
f. Have you ever had trouble at an airport? What happened?
g. What do you do when you get a stomachache?
h. Have you ever had an operation? How did you feel?

8. Learn word partnerships

Study the partnerships below. Complete the sentences so they are true for you.

LET	
let someone do something	***Airport officials let the woman board the plane.*** *My teacher lets us drink tea in class.* *I let my friend Eun-mi use my bike.* *My sister doesn't let me listen to her CDs.*

a. My English teacher lets students _____.

b. He/she doesn't let _____.

c. I let my friend _____.

9. Learn word groups

Complete the sentences so they are true for you. Use words from the pictures.

FEELING SICK

    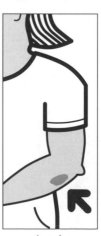 

| a stomachache | a headache | a cough | a cut | a bruise | a broken leg |

a. When I have _____, I drink tea or water.

b. I have never had _____.

c. I had _____ last year.

10. Take a dictation 🔘 track 3

Use your own paper to write the dictation. Check your answers on page 86.

11. Complete the story

Use the words from the box to complete the story.

let	cough	official	surprised
several	metal	checked	operation

A Strange Cough

TAIPEI, TAIWAN For many years, a Taiwanese man had a bad **(1)** _____. Finally, he went to see his doctor. The doctor **(2)** _____ him carefully but did not find anything wrong. **(3)** "_____ me take an X-ray," the doctor said.

The X-ray showed a piece of **(4)** _____ deep in the man's back. It was a large needle*, and it was near the man's lungs**. The man was **(5)** _____. How did the needle get there? When he told his wife about it,

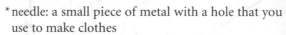

she looked surprised, too. "Oh, dear!" she said. "I remember now. I lost a needle on our bed **(6)** _____ years ago!"

A hospital **(7)** _____ said that the needle was dangerously close to the man's lungs. He had an **(8)** _____ and now the needle and the man's cough are gone.

* needle: a small piece of metal with a hole that you use to make clothes
** lungs: two parts inside your body that you use to breathe

 Talk about the stories

How are the stories of the Canadian woman and the Taiwanese man similar? How are they different?

2

Smart Guard

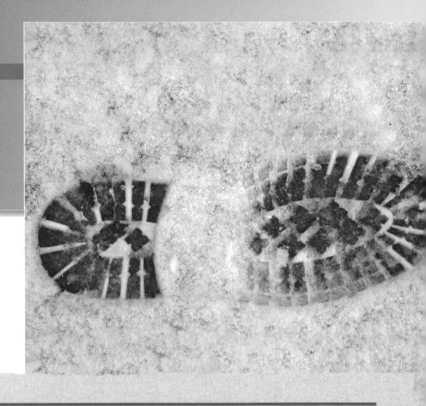

1. Read the story

Look at the pictures on these pages.
What is the story about? Now read it.

VLADIMIR, RUSSIA ¹Sergey Sokolov is a **guard** in a small town in western Russia. In the winter, he **takes care of** a group of summer homes that are empty for several months. When the **owners** are out of town, Sokolov **is responsible for** the houses. ²His job can be dangerous because there are **plenty of** thieves in the **neighborhood** who have broken into* these homes.

³Sokolov is not big or strong, but he *is* smart. One day he had a good **idea**. "I know how to keep these thieves away!" he thought. ⁴Sokolov made **extremely** large **boots** and, with big **steps**, walked in the snow all around the houses.

⁵**Clearly**, criminals have **studied** the great big footprints** because they have stayed away. ⁶Sokolov's job is much easier now. "Crime is down **almost** fifty percent***," he says. "Those footprints really **scared** them!"

---

* broken into: gone into a place by breaking a window or
  door to steal something
** footprints: marks that your feet make on the ground
*** percent: %; in each hundred

NEW WORDS

guard *n*	be responsible for *v*	idea *n*	step *n*	almost *adv*
take care of *v*	plenty of *n*	extremely *adv*	clearly *adv*	scare *v*
owner *n*	neighborhood *n*	boot *n*	study *v*	

>> See Glossary on page 88. >>

2. Rate the story

How much did you like it? Mark an **✗**.

Not at All   A Lot

① ② ③ ④ ⑤

3. Check your comprehension

Match the first and second parts of the sentences. The first one is done for you.

a. Sokolov watches a group of __4__

b. His job can be ___

c. One day he had ___

d. He made ___

e. The criminals studied ___

f. Crime is down by ___

1. an idea.

2. great big boots.

3. the large footprints.

4. summer homes.

5. almost fifty percent.

6. dangerous.

4. Check your vocabulary

Complete the sentences with the New Words.

a. When the o_ _ _ _s are away, Sokolov takes _ _ _ _ of their summer homes.

b. The neigh_ _ _ _ _ _ _ has ple_ _ _ of thieves.

c. Sokolov wanted to sc_ _ _ the criminals, so he made large b_ _ _s and took big st_ _s in the snow.

d. Cl_ _ _ly, thieves have s_ _ _ied the big footprints because they are staying away.

5. Listen to the story ◎ track 4

Now listen to the story two or three times. Look at the pictures below as you listen.

6. Retell the story

Cover the story and look at the pictures above. Retell the story using the New Words.

7. Answer the questions

About the story...
a. What is Sokolov responsible for?
b. Why is his job dangerous?
c. How did he make his job easier?
d. Do you think Sokolov enjoys his job? Why or why not?

About you...
e. Is there crime in your neighborhood? What kind?
f. How can you stop thieves from getting into your home?
g. What or who do you take care of?
h. Do you have a good idea for making your life easier? What is it?

8. Learn word partnerships

Study the partnerships below. Complete the sentences so they are true for you.

BE RESPONSIBLE FOR		
be responsible for	something or someone	**Sokolov is responsible for the houses.** I am responsible for my dog. My father is responsible for me.
	doing something	I am responsible for doing my homework. My sister is responsible for cooking dinner. We are responsible for washing the car.

a. At school, I am responsible for _____.

b. At home, I am responsible _____.

c. My teacher _____ responsible _____.

9. Learn word groups

Complete the sentences so they are true for you. Use words from the pictures.

THINGS ON YOUR FEET

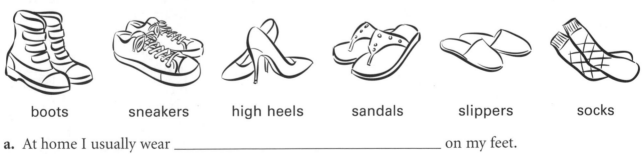

boots   sneakers   high heels   sandals   slippers   socks

a. At home I usually wear _____ on my feet.

b. In the summer, I often wear _____.

c. In the winter, I sometimes wear _____.

10. Take a dictation   track 5

Use your own paper to write the dictation. Check your answers on page 86.

11. Complete the story

Use the words from the box to complete the story.

guard	is responsible for	extremely
scares	clearly	idea

A QUEEN'S BODYGUARD

KOREA   Some people think that women cannot do dangerous jobs. But don't say that to Sun-hee Han. She is a bodyguard* for the Queen** of Jordan and **(1)** _____ keeping the queen out of danger. Han was a soldier in Korea before she went to Jordan. She is **(2)** _____ good at tae kwon do and karate. Now she is learning English and all about Islamic culture***, too.

When she was a child, Han saw a soldier and thought he looked wonderful. That gave her an **(3)** _____. She wanted to be a soldier, too. Now she loves her work as the queen's **(4)** _____. The job can be dangerous, and sometimes it **(5)** _____ her, but she is **(6)** _____ happy. "Even after I'm married, I want to do this job," she says.

_____

　*bodyguard: someone who keeps an important person out of danger
　**queen: the wife of a king
　***culture: the ideas and way of life of a group of people

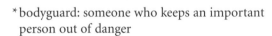 **Talk about the stories**

Which job would you like to do—Sergey Sokolov's job or Sun-hee Han's job? Why?

3

School Clothes

1. Read the story

Look at the pictures on these pages.
What is the story about? Now read it.

MORBEGNO, ITALY ¹Students at a high school near Milan were coming to class in old blue jeans with holes in the **knees**. Some of them had wild **pink** hair and nose rings. ²The **principal**, Mr. Magon, was **not at all** happy. He did not want students to wear **uniforms**, but he wanted to bring some **order** to the school. ³He sent a letter home to all **parents**. "We are going to **punish** students," he wrote, "who do not dress **suitably**."

⁴The parents met and **discussed** the school's letter. They were angry—not at their children, but at the principal! ⁵They **warned** Magon that they would take him to **court**. "Our children must be free to wear what they want at school," they **argued**.

⁶Magon was very surprised. "Some clothes are not right for school. I really thought that the parents would agree with me."

NEW WORDS

knee *n*	principal *n*	uniform *n*	parent *n*	suitably *adv*	warn *v*	argue *v*
pink *adj*	not at all *adv*	order *n*	punish *v*	discuss *v*	court *n*	

>> See Glossary on page 89. >>

2. Rate the story

How much did you like it? Mark an ✗.

Not at All   A Lot

①   ②   ③   ④   ⑤

3. Check your comprehension

Correct five more mistakes in the story summary. The first one is done for you.

Students at a ~~hospital~~ *school* in Italy were coming to class in old clothes. Some had wild hair and nose rings. The principal was not at all happy. He sent a book home to all the parents. He said that the school would punish teachers who did not dress suitably. The parents were happy. "Our children must be free to say what they want," they argued. The principal was pleased.

4. Check your vocabulary

Complete the sentences with the New Words.

a. The principal was not _ _ all happy with students' wild p_ _ _ hair.

b. He wanted to bring or_ _ _ to his school.

c. He wa_ _ _ _ parents that students must dress sui_ _ _ _ _.

d. The parents said they would take the principal to c_ _ _ _.

5. Listen to the story track 6

Now listen to the story two or three times. Look at the pictures below as you listen.

6. Retell the story

Cover the story and look at the pictures above. Retell the story using the New Words.

7. Answer the questions

About the story…

a. What didn't the principal like?

b. What did he write to the parents?

c. How did the parents reply?

d. Do you agree with the principal or the parents? Why?

About you…

e. What do you wear to school?

f. Which clothes are better for school—jeans or uniforms? Why?

g. What do your parents think about your hair and clothes?

h. What are the wildest clothes you have?

8. Learn word partnerships

Study the partnerships below. Complete the sentences so they are true for you.

DISCUSS			
discuss	a letter a book a movie a problem an idea	(with someone)	***The parents discussed the school's letter.*** *We discussed the book.* *I discussed the movie Spider-Man with my sister.* *Bill discussed the problem with his teacher.* *I like to discuss interesting ideas.*

a. In class, we often discuss _____ or _____.

b. I like to discuss _____ my friends.

c. I discussed the movie _____ with _____.

9. Learn word groups

Complete the sentences so they are true for you. Use words from the picture.

FAMILY

Anna's Family!

a. I talk like my _____.

b. I look like my _____.

c. I want to see my _____
more often.

10. Take a dictation track 7

Use your own paper to write the dictation. Check your answers on page 86.

11. Complete the story

Use the words from the box to complete the story.

grandfather	uniform	principal
discusses	knees	parents

Grandfather Gets First School Uniform

ELDORET, KENYA Kimani Maruge, 84, is going to school for the first time. Maruge is a **(1)** _____ who has gray hair and who cannot see too well. Most of the students in his class are six years old.

"I thought it was a joke* at first," the school **(2)** _____ said. "What a surprise when he arrived on the first day of school and said that he wanted to begin first grade." Maruge was wearing short blue pants above his **(3)** _____, just like the children.

Maruge helps the other students, and tells them to work hard at school and listen to their **(4)** _____. He also **(5)** _____ Kenya's history** with them. "He's like a history book," says his teacher.

Maruge wants to write a book, but first he wants to learn to read. He is the perfect student, says the principal. "He never comes to school late. He wears his **(6)** _____. And he always obeys*** us."

—————————————

* joke: something that you do or say to make people laugh
** history: all the things that happened in the past
*** obeys: does what someone tells him to do

 Talk about the stories

Imagine that you and a partner are one of the Italian students and Kimani Maruge. You are meeting for the first time. Tell each other about your life at school.

4

It's Hard to Stop!

1. Read the story

Look at the pictures on these pages.
What is the story about? Now read it.

TAIPEI, TAIWAN ¹A lot of people have **hobbies**, but who spends eight hours a day on a hobby? Meet Shi-tung Chuang. He plays online* computer **games** eight hours a day! ²Shi-tung, 19, is a **college** student at De Lin Institute. ³He does well in school, so his parents do not **mind** that he spends so much time on the computer. ⁴Does he have time for friends? "Sure, I do," he says. "All my friends have the same hobby, so we play together online. Sometimes we even see **each other** in real life!"

⁵Many online players spend too much time on their games, says Stephen Kline of Simon Fraser **University** in Canada, and this can **lead to** family fights. Some players are addicted**, he **adds**.
⁶"I'm not addicted," says Shi-tung, "**although** it is **a bit** hard to stop. It's **crazy** and so much **fun** to play. I want to **succeed**! I want to win!"

* online: on the Internet
** addicted: not able to stop doing something bad

NEW WORDS

hobby *n*	mind *v*	lead to *v*	a bit *mod*	succeed *v*
game *n*	each other *pron*	add *v*	crazy *adj*	
college *n*	university *n*	although *conj*	fun *n*	

>> See Glossary on page 89. >>

2. Rate the story

How much did you like it? Mark an ✗.

Not at All   A Lot
① ② ③ ④ ⑤

3. Check your comprehension

Check (✔) the endings that are true. The first one is done for you.

a. Shi-tung plays games

  ✓ for many hours each day.

  ___ on his computer.

  ___ with his parents.

  ___ with Stephen Kline.

  ___ because they are fun.

b. Some online players

  ___ have fights with their families.

  ___ are addicted to games.

  ___ think that it is hard to stop.

  ___ spend too much time on games.

4. Check your vocabulary

Complete the sentences with the New Words.

a. Shi-tung's parents don't m_ _ _ that he spends so much time on his

ho_ _ _ because he does well in col_ _ _ _.

b. Shi-tung says that he is not addicted, alth_ _ _ _ it is a _ _ _ hard to stop playing.

c. When Shi-tung plays an online game, he wants to su_ _ _ _ _ _.

d. "It's cr_ _ _ and so much f_ _!" he says.

5. Listen to the story track 8

Now listen to the story two or three times. Look at the pictures below as you listen.

6. Retell the story

Cover the story and look at the pictures above. Retell the story using the New Words.

7. Answer the questions

About the story…

a. How does Shi-tung spend his day?

b. How do his parents feel about his hobby?

c. Why is it hard for Shi-tung to stop playing?

d. Do you think he spends too much time playing? Why or why not?

About you…

e. What computer games have you played? Which is your favorite?

f. What are your hobbies?

g. How much time do you spend each week on your hobbies?

h. How often do you and your friends see each other?

8. Learn word partnerships

Study the partnerships below. Complete the sentences so they are true for you.

FUN	
It is (so much) fun to do (something)	**It's so much fun to play.** It's fun to spend time with my friends. It's so much fun to ride a horse!
have (a lot of) fun	I will have fun this weekend. We had a lot of fun at the party. I had fun when I went to Australia.

a. It is so much fun _____!

b. I will _____ fun _____.

c. I had a lot of fun when _____.

9. Learn word groups

Complete the sentences so they are true for you. Use words from the pictures.

GAMES

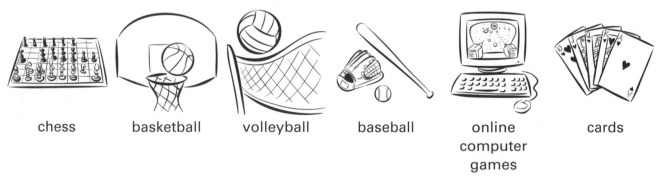

chess basketball volleyball baseball online computer games cards

a. I think that playing _____ is so much fun.

b. I never play _____.

c. I want to learn to play _____.

10. Take a dictation 💿 track 9

Use your own paper to write the dictation. Check your answers on page 86.

11. Complete the story

Use the words from the box to complete the story.

lead	university	adds	games	each other	fun to talk

Addicted!

RAGUSA, ITALY   Simona Barone, a **(1)** _____ student in Italy, is addicted to her cell phone. Like many people, she carries it with her almost everywhere. "My friends and I like to talk to **(2)** _____ all the time," she says. Simona even sleeps with her phone at night. "I always think that my friends from around the world will call me," she says. She plays **(3)** _____ on her phone before she falls asleep. Her friend Davide Fiorito feels the same way about his phone. "It's like a part of me!" he says.

Although it is **(4)** _____ on cell phones, they can **(5)** _____ to trouble. "I talk a bit too much," Simona says. "It's expensive and my father gets angry." Simona **(6)** _____ that she is obsessive* about checking her messages**. When she is out with friends, she cannot stop checking her phone—which does not please her friends!

* obsessive: thinking about something all the time
** messages: words that people send to one another

  Talk about the stories

Shi-tung Chuang and Simona Barone spend most of their day with technology. How about you? Do you spend too much time with technology? Why or why not?

5

Stuck in the Mud

1. Read the story

Look at the pictures on these pages.
What is the story about? Now read it.

BRIDGEWATER, MASS., USA **¹**One winter day, Mike Hill was **hunting** for birds near a **lake**. The ground was wet, and his boots got stuck* in the **mud**. He could not get out. **²**Hill quickly **became** cold and **scared**, and he phoned for help.

³First, three fire fighters came to **save** Hill but had no **success**. They tried to get to him by boat, but their **engine** got stuck in the mud. So they tried to walk to Hill, but their boots got stuck. Now no one **was able to** move! **⁴**Then a policeman and a dog came in a special car with large wheels. It got stuck, too.

⁵Finally, a **helicopter** arrived to save the day. It pulled everyone up from the mud **safely**. **One by one**, Hill, the fire fighters, the policeman, and the dog went up through the trees in a muddy **basket**. **⁶**"It was a pretty big **mess**," said the helicopter **pilot**.

---

*stuck: cannot move

NEW WORDS

hunt *v*	**become** *v*	**success** *n*	**helicopter** *n*	**basket** *n*
lake *n*	**scared** *adj*	**engine** *n*	**safely** *adv*	**mess** *n*
mud *n*	**save** *v*	**be able to** *v*	**one by one** *adv*	**pilot** *n*

>> See Glossary on page 90. >>

2. Rate the story

How much did you like it? Mark an ✗.

Not at All   A Lot

① ② ③ ④ ⑤

3. Check your comprehension

Put the sentences in the correct order. Number them 1–6.

a. ___ His boots got stuck.

b. ___ Hill was hunting near a lake.

c. ___ A helicopter arrived.

d. ___ He was scared and called for help.

e. ___ It pulled everyone up in a muddy basket.

f. ___ Fire fighters and a policeman got stuck, too.

4. Check your vocabulary

Complete the sentences with the New Words.

a. Hill was _ _ _ _ing for birds when he got stuck in the _ _ _.

b. He was not _ _ _ _ to move and be_ _ _ _ cold.

c. Fire fighters had no suc_ _ _ _ when they tried to s_ _ _ Hill.

d. The eng_ _ _ of their boat got stuck, and they did, too.

e. Finally, a helicopter pi_ _ _ pulled everyone up in a b_ _ _ _ _.

5. Listen to the story track 10

Now listen to the story two or three times. Look at the pictures below as you listen.

6. Retell the story

Cover the story and look at the pictures above. Retell the story using the New Words.

7. Answer the questions

About the story...
a. What was Hill doing near the lake?
b. Why did he phone for help?
c. Who came to save him?
d. How did the helicopter pull everyone up?

About you...
e. Would you like to ride in a helicopter? Why or why not?
f. Think of a time when you were scared. What happened?
g. Have you ever been in a big mess? What happened?
h. Many people hunt. What do you think of the sport?

8. Learn word partnerships

Study the partnerships below. Complete the sentences so they are true for you.

MESS		
be make clean up	a (terrible / big / huge) mess	***It was a pretty big mess.*** *My closet is a terrible mess.* *We made a huge mess when we cooked.* *Joni often makes a mess in the car.* *I need to clean up the mess on my desk.* *Please clean up that terrible mess!*

a. _____ is a _____ mess.
b. I made _____ mess when _____.
c. I need to _____ the mess in/on _____.

9. Learn word groups

Complete the sentences so they are true for you. Use words from the pictures.

FEELINGS

scared   confused   delighted   bored   excited   sad

a. I'm sometimes _____ when I watch sports on TV.
b. When an old friend calls, I feel _____.
c. When I speak English, I'm sometimes _____.
d. I'm _____ when I play computer games.

10. Take a dictation 💿 track 11

Use your own paper to write the dictation. Check your answers on page 86.

11. Complete the story

Use the words from the box to complete the story.

scared	saved	lake	were not able to
safely	mud	a terrible mess	

MEN GET STUCK IN A LAKE

SALISBURY, N.C., USA   Two young men in North Carolina got stuck in the mud while they were running away from police. Kevin Chawlk, 17, and Richard Neri, 20, were driving their car too fast, so two policemen began to follow them. Then the men became **(1)** _____ and drove even faster. The car finally crashed into a tree. The men jumped out and began to run across a muddy area near a **(2)** _____. The weather was very cold, and one man was only wearing pants and a T-shirt. Both men lost their shoes and got stuck in the cold **(3)** _____. They **(4)** _____ move.

It took police three hours, but they got the men out **(5)** _____. It was **(6)** _____! "We **(7)** _____ them, so they didn't die from the cold," a policeman said. "They weren't too smart!"

Talk about the stories

How are the stories of Mike Hill and the two young men, Kevin Chawlk and Richard Neri, similar? How are they different?

6

Cops on Wheels

1. Read the story

Look at the pictures on these pages.
What is the story about? Now read it.

PARIS, FRANCE **¹**What is your idea of a **cool** job? Would you like to spend the day on **in-line skates** in the **lovely** streets of Paris? That is what a group of French **police officers** do. In their blue uniforms, they **speed** through Paris traffic on in-line skates. **²Look out!** They **chase** thieves and try to **catch up with** them. They give tickets to drivers who are talking on cell phones.

³It is a very good job. The cops* **skate** only four hours a day, four days a week. **⁴**The rest of the time they go to the gym** because they have to stay **in shape** for this job. **⁵**But it can be dangerous—the streets are not always **flat**. No officer has **seriously** hurt himself yet, but some have taken a bad fall.

⁶Young French women like the cops on wheels, and **tourists** love them, too. "I'm in thousands of Japanese photos!" says one cop.

---

* cops (informal): policemen or policewomen
** gym: a place where you exercise and do sports.

NEW WORDS

cool (informal) *adj*	**police officer** *n*	**chase** *v*	**in shape** *adv*	**tourist** *n*
in-line skate *n*	**speed** *v*	**catch up with** *v*	**flat** *adj*	
lovely *adj*	**look out** *v*	**skate** *v*	**seriously** *adv*	

>> See Glossary on page 90. >>

2. Rate the story

How much did you like it? Mark an ✗.

Not at All   A Lot
①   ②   ③   ④   ⑤

3. Check your comprehension

Match the first and second parts of the sentences.

a. The French cops speed through ___   **1.** in shape for the job.

b. They chase criminals and give ___   **2.** traffic on in-line skates.

c. They stay ___   **3.** dangerous.

d. Their work can be ___   **4.** photos of the cops.

e. Tourists take ___   **5.** tickets to drivers.

4. Check your vocabulary

Complete the sentences with the New Words.

a. A group of police off_ _ _ _ _ move through Paris on in-line sk_ _ _ _.

b. They sp_ _ _ through the lov_ _ _ streets.

c. They ch_ _ _ thieves and c_ _ _ _ up with them.

d. The streets are not always f_ _ _, but no cop has been ser_ _ _ _ _ _ hurt yet.

5. Listen to the story   track 12

Now listen to the story two or three times. Look at the pictures below as you listen.

6. Retell the story

Cover the story and look at the pictures above. Retell the story using the New Words.

7. Answer the questions

About the story…

a. What work do these Paris cops do?

b. What are the good and bad sides of the job?

c. Why do tourists take their photo?

d. Would you like this job? Why or why not?

About you…

e. What three jobs do you think are cool? Why?

f. When do you think it is *not* OK to talk on a cell phone?

g. Have you ever skated? Is it a good way to stay in shape? Why or why not?

h. What do tourists take photos of in your country?

8. Learn word partnerships

Study the partnerships below. Complete the sentences so they are true for you.

IN SHAPE		
stay get be	in shape	**The cops have to stay in shape for this job.** *I'd like to get in shape for summer.* *He's in shape because he plays tennis.*
in	perfect good bad	shape	*Sports star David Beckham is in perfect shape.* *Motoko was in good shape last year.* *I'm in bad shape because I never go to the gym.*

a. My favorite sports star, _____, is _____ shape.

b. My friend _____ shape.

c. I'm _____ shape because _____.

9. Learn word groups

Complete the sentences so they are true for you. Use words from the picture.

THINGS WITH WHEELS

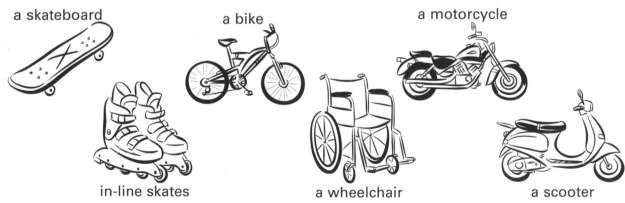

a skateboard · a bike · a motorcycle · in-line skates · a wheelchair · a scooter

a. When I was younger I had _____.

b. I want to buy _____.

c. My friends have _____ and _____.

10. Take a dictation 💿 track 13

Use your own paper to write the dictation. Check your answers on page 86.

11. Complete the story

Use the words from the box to complete the story.

| wheelchair | speeds | cool | in perfect shape | seriously | look out |

PRINCIPAL ON WHEELS

DAEJEON, KOREA **(1)** _____! Here comes the principal! Yong-gyun Oh **(2)** _____ around his school in Korea. His students call him "Principal in a **(3)** _____."

A few years ago, Mr. Oh opened a school for children with disabilities*. Little by little, Mr. Oh said, he began to understand something important. People with disabilities have so much to give to the world.

Mr. Oh's students think that he is a **(4)** _____ principal, and Mr. Oh is surprised at his new life. Ten years ago, he was wearing an air force** uniform, and he was **(5)** _____. Then he became **(6)** _____ ill and could not walk any more. Dark and angry days followed, but then Mr. Oh had the idea to open a school for people like himself. He became happy.

Now his friends envy*** him because he has a full life. "I am living a very fruitful life," the principal says, "in a very new world."

---

* disabilities: serious problems people have with their bodies
** air force: the airplanes and people that a country uses for fighting
*** envy: want what another person has

 Talk about the stories

Imagine that you and a partner are a "cop on wheels" and Yong-gyun Oh. You are meeting for the first time. Tell each other about your life on wheels.

1. Match the words with the pictures.

___ **a.** guard

___ **b.** knee

___ **c.** court

___ **d.** engine

___ **e.** uniform

___ **f.** coin

___ **g.** basket

___ **h.** instrument

1.

2.

3.

4.

5.

6.

7.

8.

2. Write the words in the picture.

lake	boots	mud	in-line skates	game
tourist	police officer	parents		

3. Are the sentences true or false? Check (✔) the correct box.

                                           T   F

a. A helicopter has an engine. ☐ ☐

b. People have four knees. ☐ ☐

c. A principal works in a court. ☐ ☐

d. The world is flat. ☐ ☐

e. Police officers can give tickets to people who speed. ☐ ☐

f. Coins are made of metal. ☐ ☐

g. You have an operation in a hospital. ☐ ☐

4. Cross out the item that *cannot* complete each sentence.

a. When Bob got on the horse, he was _____ scared.

    1. not at all   2. a bit   3. extremely   4. safely

b. The prison officials _____ the criminals.

    1. searched   2. punished   3. chased   4. succeeded

c. The children had fun playing with _____.

    1. the game   2. each other   3. the tourists   4. success

d. Naomi was wearing a _____ hat.

    1. lovely   2. cool   3. crazy   4. surprised

e. I am _____ my little sister.

    1. taking care of   2. speeding through   3. skating with   4. responsible for

5. Match the words with the definitions.

a. catch up with ____   1. to be careful

b. order ____   2. very good, with nothing wrong

c. save ____   3. when you move your foot up and put it down in another place, you take one of these

d. step ____   4. to tell someone about danger or about something bad that will happen

e. perfect ____   5. to take someone or something away from danger

f. mess ____   6. when everyone is doing the right thing or everything is in the right place

g. warn ____   7. to move quickly so that you are not behind someone

h. look out ____   8. something dirty or a big problem

6. Use the words from the box to complete the sentences.

suitably	studied	one by one	flat	seriously	warned
checked	clearly	lead to	safely	adds	let	University

a. When the officials at the airport _____ the Canadian woman, they found nothing, so they _____ her pass.

b. _____, criminals have _____ Sokolov's big footprints because they have stayed away.

c. Mr. Magon _____ parents that students had to dress _____ for school.

d. Stephen Kline of Simon Fraser _____ says that computer games can _____ family fights. Some players are addicted, he _____.

e. _____, a helicopter pilot pulled all the muddy people up _____.

f. The Paris streets are not always _____, but none of the Paris cops has _____ hurt himself yet.

7. Use the words from the box to complete the story.

idea	games	although	take care of	not at all	boarded	lovely

Woman, 82, Loves Living on Water

SOUTHAMPTON, ENGLAND

Five years ago, Beatrice Muller, 82, **(1)** _____ a large cruise ship* and began traveling around the world. The woman says that the ship, the QE2, is now her home, and she plans to live on it for the rest of her life. "It's **(2)** _____ and no more expensive than living in a home for old people," she says.

Muller got the **(3)** _____ after her husband died. She says that a ship is the perfect place to live. She plays **(4)** _____, dances, or just sits in the sun. There are people on the ship who **(5)** _____ her. There is plenty of good food.

"This is where I live and I love it," says Muller. **(6)** _____ she is far from her family, she is **(7)** _____ lonely. She has made friends and uses e-mail to talk to family.

*cruise ship: a ship for tourists

8. Check (✔) yes or no.

	Yes	No
a. I always try to stay in shape.	☐	☐
b. My neighborhood is extremely clean.	☐	☐
c. I am responsible for doing the dishes at home.	☐	☐
d. Dogs scare me.	☐	☐
e. I like to board the plane early when I fly.	☐	☐
f. I often argue with my friends.	☐	☐
g. I would like to hunt.	☐	☐
h. I go to college.	☐	☐
i. My parents often punished me when I was younger.	☐	☐

9. Complete the sentences so they are true for you.

a. I am scared when _____.

b. I think that _____ is fun.

c. I would like to become _____.

d. My hobby is _____.

e. I have plenty of _____.

f. Yesterday, I discussed _____ with _____.

g. When I was young, my parents did not let me _____.

h. When I have a stomachache, I drink _____.

10. Fill in the chart with names of classmates. Try to write a different name in each blank. Walk around the room and ask questions such as:

Do you have several animals?
Are you able to skate?

The winner is the first person to fill in seven blanks.

FIND SOMEONE WHO...

a. has several animals. _____

b. is able to skate. _____

c. has an interesting hobby. _____

d. reads almost two books a month. _____

e. lives near a lake. _____

f. wears a lot of pink clothes. _____

g. often makes a mess. _____

h. would like to be a pilot. _____

i. passes a garden on the way to school. _____

j. doesn't mind making dinner. _____

7

Try a Little Kindness

1. Read the story

Look at the pictures on these pages.
What is the story about? Now read it.

SINGAPORE [1]Is our world becoming a colder and **less** friendly place? Maybe it is, but Singapore is trying hard to change that. The country has **joined** the World **Kindness** Movement*. [2]This movement started at a meeting** in Tokyo in 1997. Now Japan, Korea, Australia, Canada, the USA, and several other countries belong to the group, which wants to **spread** kindness around the world.

[3]How can people like you and me make life more **pleasant** for everyone? The Singapore Kindness Movement has some **excellent** ideas. [4]For example, the group says, wash someone's car as a surprise. [5]At home, try to spend a little time every day with your parents and grandparents. And don't **bother** your **neighbors** with loud music—**turn down** your **stereo** after 10 P.M. [6]At school, **invite** a new student to **share** your lunch. [7]Don't **throw** litter*** in the streets—try to **pick up** papers and bottles! [8]And finally, don't forget to smile, smile, smile!

---

*movement: a group of people who have the same ideas
**meeting: a time when people come together to talk
***litter: pieces of paper and other things that people leave on the ground

NEW WORDS

less *adv*	kindness *n*	pleasant *adj*	bother *v*	turn down *v*	invite *v*	throw *v*
join *v*	spread *v*	excellent *adj*	neighbor *n*	stereo *n*	share *v*	pick up *v*

>> See Glossary on page 91. >>

2. Rate the story

How much did you like it? Mark an ✗.

Not at All   A Lot

①　②　③　④　⑤

3. Check your comprehension

Check (✔) the endings that are true.

a. Singapore

___ wants to make the world a colder place.

___ wants to spread kindness.

___ has joined the World Kindness Movement.

___ has ideas to make life more pleasant for people.

b. The movement wants people

___ to bother their neighbors.

___ to be nice to new students.

___ to throw litter in the streets.

___ to smile more.

4. Check your vocabulary

Complete the sentences with the New Words.

a. Singapore has j_ _ _ed the World Kind_ _ _ _ Movement and wants to make the world a l_ _ _ cold place.

b. The people in the movement have some ex_ _ _ _ _ _ _ ideas.

c. Don't bo_ _ _ _ your nei_ _ _ _ _s. Turn _ _ _ _ your loud music!

d. P_ _ _ up litter on the streets.

5. Listen to the story track 14

Now listen to the story two or three times. Look at the pictures below as you listen.

6. Retell the story

Cover the story and look at the pictures above. Retell the story using the New Words.

7. Answer the questions

About the story...
a. Which countries belong to the World Kindness Movement?
b. What does the group want to do?
c. Which of Singapore's ideas do you like best? Why?
d. Do you think Singapore will succeed and make the world a friendlier place? Why or why not?

About you...
e. How can you spread kindness at your school?
f. What do you do to make life pleasant for your family?
g. What do you do that bothers your family or your neighbors?
h. What bothers you? Why?

8. Learn word partnerships

Study the partnerships below. Complete the sentences so they are true for you.

INVITE		
invite someone	to do something	***Invite a new student to share your lunch!*** *I invited John to see a movie.* *My friends invited us to go to the beach.*
	to something	*They invited me to a party.* *I would like to invite a friend to dinner.* *Pei-ting often invites me to his house.*

a. Last year, I invited _____ to _____.

b. I would like to invite _____ to _____.

c. _____ invited me _____.

9. Learn word groups

Complete the sentences so they are true for you. Use words from the picture.

MUSIC

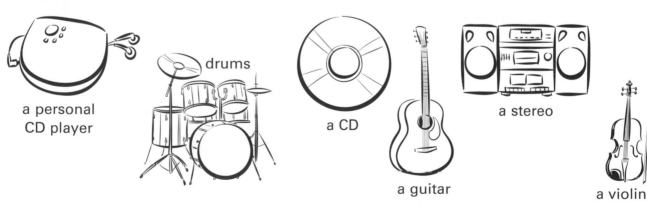

a personal CD player

drums

a CD

a guitar

a stereo

a violin

a. I have _____ at home.

b. I would like to learn to play _____.

c. I want to buy _____.

10. Take a dictation track 15

Use your own paper to write the dictation. Check your answers on page 86.

11. Complete the story

Use the words from the box to complete the story.

neighbors	bother	kindness	threw
spread	pleasant	share	pick up

↑An Act of Kindness↓

NAGOYA, JAPAN   After he made a lot of money in the stock market*, a Japanese man wanted to **(1)** _____ some with his **(2)** _____. The unnamed man took two large bags of money to the top floor of a tall building in Nagoya. Then he took handfuls of bills—about $9,000—and **(3)** _____ them from an open window. The money rained down, and then the wind **(4)** _____ it around the streets—a **(5)** _____ surprise for everyone! People ran to **(6)** _____ the money.

Later, the 26-year-old man went on Japanese television and said that he had too much money. "I don't need it," he said. "I wanted to give some back to the world."

The man's act** of **(7)** _____ did not **(8)** _____ the police. "He did not break any laws,***" said a police officer.

_____

* stock market: the business of buying and selling shares in companies
** act: something that you do
*** laws: rules of a country that say what people can and cannot do

 Talk about the stories

Which act of kindness from the two stories would you like to try? Why? What are two more ways to spread kindness in your town?

8

Girls Save Falling Child

1. Read the story

Look at the pictures on these pages.
What is the story about? Now read it.

BARRIE, CANADA [1]Police have **congratulated** two young Canadian girls for their quick thinking*. [2]Nine-year-old Stephanie Boddy and her friend Samantha Quinn were enjoying a **calm** afternoon **outdoors**. [3]The girls were sitting on the **grass** near their **apartment** building and having a picnic** on an old **blanket**.

[4]They looked up to see a four-year-old boy, Skyler Christou, who was falling from a fourth floor window. [5]Without **hesitating**, Stephanie and Samantha pulled the blanket from under their picnic and ran to catch the child. [6]**As** the child fell, he turned **over and over**. The two girls held their blanket open **wide**. "We moved **back and forth** as he came down," Stephanie said. "I was really scared."

[7]Skyler fell into the center of the blanket, bounced*** up, and then fell onto the ground. He was not seriously hurt. The blanket saved him. [8]Samantha's mother said that she **was proud of** the girls. And the Barrie police **chief** added, "They're wonderful!"

---

* thinking: the idea that they had
** picnic: a meal that you eat outside
*** bounced: moved up quickly after hitting something

NEW WORDS

congratulate *v*	**grass** *n*	**hesitate** *v*	**wide** *adv*	**chief** *n*
calm *adj*	**apartment** *n*	**as** *conj*	**back and forth** *adv*	
outdoors *adv*	**blanket** *n*	**over and over** *adv*	**be proud of** *v*	

>> See Glossary on page 91. >>

2. Rate the story

How much did you like it? Mark an ✗.

Not at All   A Lot

(1) (2) (3) (4) (5)

3. Check your comprehension

Put the sentences in the correct order. Number them 1–7.

a. ___ The boy fell into the blanket.

b. ___ They did not hesitate.

c. ___ They moved back and forth with their blanket open wide.

d. ___ They looked up at their apartment building.

e. ___ The police chief congratulated the girls for their good work.

f. ___ They saw a small boy who was falling.

g. ___ Two girls were having a picnic outdoors.

4. Check your vocabulary

Complete the sentences with the New Words.

a. The girls were having a picnic on the g_ _ _ _ on a c_ _ _ afternoon.

b. The girls did not hes_ _ _ _ _ when they saw the boy falling from the window of his apar_ _ _ _ _ _.

c. A_ the boy turned o_ _ _ and o_ _ _, the girls opened their blanket w_ _ _.

d. Samantha's mother was pr_ _ _ of the girls.

5. Listen to the story 🔘 track 16

Now listen to the story two or three times. Look at the pictures below as you listen.

6. Retell the story

Cover the story and look at the pictures above. Retell the story using the New Words.

7. Answer the questions

About the story…
a. Why did the police chief congratulate the girls?
b. What were the girls doing when they first saw Skyler?
c. What happened to the boy as he fell?
d. What saved him?

About you…
e. Where do you like to have a picnic?
f. Have you or your friends ever been in danger? What happened?
g. Who have you congratulated and for what?
h. Which famous person from your country are you proud of? Why?

8. Learn word partnerships

Study the partnerships below. Complete the sentences so they are true for you.

BE PROUD OF		
be proud of	something or someone	***Samantha's mother is proud of the girls.*** *My parents are proud of me.* *I'm proud of my schoolwork.*
	doing something	*I'm proud of playing the guitar well.* *She's proud of doing well in school.* *We're proud of winning the game.*

a. _____ proud of me.

b. I'm proud of _____.

c. When I was a child, I was proud _____.

9. Learn word groups

Answer the questions so they are true. Use words from the picture.

OUTDOORS

a tree

a cloud

a bush

grass

a branch

a rock

a. What can you find in the sky?
b. What can you find near the sea?
c. What can you find near your house?

10. Take a dictation track 17

Use your own paper to write the dictation. Check your answers on page 86.

11. Complete the story

Use the words from the box to complete the story.

as	branch	grass	outdoors
back and forth		is proud of	

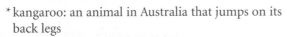

Kangaroo Saves Man's Life

MORWELL, AUSTRALIA   A family in Australia **(1)** _____ their kangaroo*, Lulu. The wonderful animal saved the life of their father, Len Richards, 52.

(2) _____ Richards was walking **(3)** _____ near his home, a tree **(4)** _____ broke and knocked the man to the ground. He was seriously hurt. When Lulu found Richards, she barked** like a dog and went to find the family. She ran **(5)** _____ until the family followed her. "Lulu is never like that," said Celeste Richards, 17, "so we knew something was wrong with my father."

The kangaroo stood guard in the long **(6)** _____ next to Richards until help came. Richards does not remember the accident, but his family has told him what Lulu did. "I love that kangaroo; she saved my life," he says. Lulu finds herself food in the Richards' kitchen when she is hungry, so they always knew that the animal was smart. But they did not think that she was that smart! Now she is also famous.

———————————

* kangaroo: an animal in Australia that jumps on its back legs

** barked: made a noise like a dog

 Talk about the stories

How are the stories of the two Canadian girls and Lulu similar? How are they different?

9

The Wedding Dress

1. Read the story

Look at the pictures on these pages.
What is the story about? Now read it.

NORTHMOOR, MO., USA ¹Dan and Jennifer Wells were planning a May **wedding**. ²Before the big day, they bought a 50-year-old house with big trees all around and were busy **repairing** it—**fixing** the walls and **cleaning** the floors. ³There was a little workshop* **nearby**. Jennifer **hung** her beautiful white wedding dress there to keep it **clean**.

⁴Three days before the wedding, while Dan and Jennifer were at his family's home, a wild tornado** came out of nowhere. ⁵The tornado missed his family's home, but when Dan drove to his house, it was not there. The trees **as well as** the neighbors' houses were gone. The tornado **destroyed** almost everything in the neighborhood. ⁶Just one thing was still standing—the workshop. When Dan looked inside, he **discovered** the wedding dress, untouched. ⁷He called Jennifer. "Your dress is here!" he told her. "I think our wedding is meant to be***."

⁸The lucky **couple** cried at their wedding. "They're **grateful** to be here," explained a friend.

---

* workshop: a place where people make things
** tornado: very strong winds that move in a circle
*** is meant to be: is supposed to happen

NEW WORDS

wedding *n*	**fix** *v*	**nearby** *adv*	**clean** *adj*	**destroy** *v*	**couple** *n*
repair *v*	**clean** *v*	**hang** *v*	**as well as** *conj*	**discover** *v*	**grateful** *adj*

>> See Glossary on page 92. >>

2. Rate the story

How much did you like it? Mark an ✗.

Not at All   A Lot
①   ②   ③   ④   ⑤

3. Check your comprehension

Match the first and second parts of the sentences.

a. Dan and Jennifer were planning ___	**1.** an old house.
b. They were repairing ___	**2.** nowhere.
c. Jennifer hung ___	**3.** was not touched.
d. A tornado came out of ___	**4.** their wedding.
e. It destroyed ___	**5.** her dress nearby in a workshop.
f. The wedding dress ___	**6.** their house and neighborhood.

4. Check your vocabulary

Complete the sentences with the New Words.

a. Dan and Jennifer were cl_ _ _ing the floors in their house before their May we_ _ _ _ _.

b. Jennifer wanted to keep her dress c_ _ _ _, so she h_ _ _ it in a little workshop.

c. Then their home as _ _ _ _ as their neighbors' homes were de_ _ _ _yed by a tornado.

d. The cou_ _ _ felt gra_ _ _ _ _ to be alive on their wedding day.

5. Listen to the story track 18

Now listen to the story two or three times. Look at the pictures below as you listen.

6. Retell the story

Cover the story and look at the pictures above. Retell the story using the New Words.

7. Answer the questions

About the story…

a. What were Dan and Jennifer doing to the house before the wedding?

b. What did the tornado destroy? What did it miss?

c. What did Dan tell Jennifer when he discovered the dress?

d. Why do you think the couple cried at their wedding?

About you…

e. Has a storm ever destroyed part of your country? What happened?

f. What do you need to fix in your home?

g. What are you grateful for?

h. Have you ever discovered something wonderful? What was it?

8. Learn word partnerships

Study the partnerships below. Complete the sentences so they are true for you.

HANG			
hang	a dress	on a hanger	***Jennifer hung her wedding dress nearby.***
	a coat		*I never hang my coat on a hanger.*
	pants		*She hung her pants carefully on the hanger.*
	a hat	on a hook	*I usually hang my hat on the hook.*
	an umbrella		*Please hang your umbrella on the hook.*
	a shirt	in a closet	*He hung his shirt in the closet.*

a. I usually hang my pants _____.

b. I never hang _____ in the closet.

c. I always hang my _____ carefully _____.

9. Learn word groups

Complete the sentences so they are true. Use words from the picture.

A WEDDING

a photographer a groom a bride

a ring

a wedding cake

a wedding dress

a. At a wedding, the bride and groom give each other _____.

b. _____ takes pictures of the couple.

c. _____ wears a wedding dress.

d. _____ is sometimes tall and white, and often tastes good.

10. Take a dictation 💿 track 19

Use your own paper to write the dictation. Check your answers on page 86.

11. Complete the story

Use the words from the box to complete the story.

bride	wedding	nearby	groom
wedding cake	couples	discovered	

Dancing with Mickey

ORLANDO, USA   "This was always my dream*," says Sachiko Takahashi, 26. Sachiko just had her **(1)** _____ at Walt Disney World Resort. While she and her new husband were eating their **(2)** _____, Mickey Mouse and Minnie Mouse ran into the room. "Mickey!" screamed an excited Sachiko. Mickey danced with Sachiko as Minnie danced **(3)** _____ with the **(4)** _____. Mickey and Minnie had big shoes, and it was hard to dance, but no one minded.

Many people have **(5)** _____ that they can get married at Walt Disney World Resort. There are about 2,000 weddings there each year. **(6)** _____ can marry in Cinderella's castle**. The **(7)** _____ can ride in Cinderella's coach*** while the groom rides on a white horse. But it is all very expensive. Couples will pay $2,500 to use Cinderella's coach for two hours, and $1,300 to spend an hour with Mickey.

_____

   * dream: something nice that you hope for
  ** castle: a large, old building where kings and queens live
*** coach: a kind of car with four wheels that horses pull

 Talk about the stories

Imagine that you and a partner are Dan Wells and Sachiko Takahashi. You are meeting for the first time. Tell each other about your weddings.

10

A Worm a Day

1. Read the story

Look at the pictures on these pages.
What is the story about? Now read it.

NAKHON NAYOK, THAILAND [1]People around the world eat different unusual foods. Some eat **insects** like grasshoppers* or flies. [2]Paisit Chanta, 39, eats something unusual, too—a worm** a day!

[3]His **habit** began 30 years ago while he was sitting in a boat and waiting for a fish to **bite**. There was nothing to eat in the boat, and he got hungry. [4]Chanta looked at his **can** of worms. "Suddenly, I **realized** that fish don't die from eating worms," he said later, "so I won't **either**." [5]Chanta ate them one by one, until he felt full. They weren't bad!

[6]Now Chanta **is crazy about** worms and thinks they are like **medicine**. "I eat a worm a day to stay **healthy**," he says. [7]Chanta works as a fire fighter and often **digs** for worms near the fire station. "We **are used to** that," says a coworker***, but we still think it is strange."

[8]Chanta does not **care** what others think. "To me, the worms taste just like rice!"

---

  * grasshoppers: insects that jump high with long back legs
  ** worm: a small animal with a long, thin body and no legs
 *** coworker: a person who works with you

NEW WORDS

insect *n*	bite *v*	realize *v*	be crazy about *v*	healthy *adj*	be used to *v*
habit *n*	can *n*	either *adv*	medicine *n*	dig *v*	care *v*

>> See Glossary on page 92. >>

2. Rate the story

How much did you like it? Mark an ✗.

Not at All   A Lot
①   ②   ③   ④   ⑤

3. Check your comprehension

Correct five mistakes in the story summary.

Many years ago, Paisit Chanta was sitting in a car and waiting for a dog to bite. He suddenly got tired, so he decided to eat some worms. They were not bad! Chanta now eats one worm a week. He says that worms keep him healthy and taste just like chocolate!

4. Check your vocabulary

Complete the sentences with the New Words.

a. Chanta's unusual ha_ _ _ started while he was waiting for a fish to b_ _ _.

b. He looked at his c_ _ of worms. "Fish don't die from eating worms," he re_ _ _zed, "so I won't eit_ _ _."

c. Chanta often d_ _s for worms, and he takes them like medi_ _ _ _.

d. "We are u_ _ _ to that," says his coworker.

5. Listen to the story track 20

Now listen to the story two or three times. Look at the pictures below as you listen.

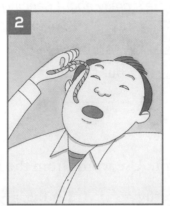

6. Retell the story

Cover the story and look at the pictures above. Retell the story using the New Words.

7. Answer the questions

About the story…

a. When and why did Chanta's habit begin?

b. What does he think worms do for him?

c. What do his coworkers think about the unusual habit?

d. What do you think about it?

About you…

e. What unusual foods do you or your friends eat?

f. Which foods were strange to you as a child? Are you used to them now?

g. What foods are you crazy about?

h. What healthy and unhealthy foods do you eat?

8. Learn word partnerships

Study the partnerships below. Complete the sentences so they are true for you.

BE CRAZY ABOUT		
be (really) crazy about	something	***Chanta is crazy about worms.*** *I'm really crazy about cats.* *She's crazy about pop music.*
	doing something	*I'm really crazy about traveling.* *He's crazy about dancing.*

a. I don't like _____, but I'm crazy about _____.

b. My friend _____ crazy about _____, but I'm not.

c. I'm not crazy _____.

9. Learn word groups

Complete the sentences so they are true for you. Use words from the picture.

a. Sometimes I find _____ in my house.

b. When I see _____, I feel scared.

c. I think _____ is a beautiful insect.

10. Take a dictation track 21

Use your own paper to write the dictation. Check your answers on page 86.

11. Complete the story

Use the words from the box to complete the story.

digs	habit	insect	worms
is crazy about		crickets	healthy

Crazy About Scorpions

SAN FRANCISCO, USA   Have you ever eaten an **(1)** _____? Scott Bowers, 32, **(2)** _____ them. His unusual **(3)** _____ began in 1999. He was spending time in the country on a business trip, and he was bored. So he chased and caught some big black **(4)** _____ and cooked them for his coworkers. They were very tasty!

What is Bowers' favorite food? Scorpions! "They taste like fish," he says. He also likes **(5)** _____. He **(6)** _____ them up from the ground and cooks them with vegetables.

Bowers likes the taste of insects, but he also eats them because they are **(7)** _____. Bowers shares his hobby with other insect-lovers in his neighborhood. He goes out with them to restaurants that have insects on the menu. Bowers has also made a Website for people who enjoy eating insects and are looking for new recipes*.

_____
* recipes: pieces of writing that tell you how to cook something

Talk about the stories

Imagine that you and a partner are Paisit Chanta and Scott Bowers. You are meeting for the first time. Tell each other what you like to eat.

11

Miracle Woman

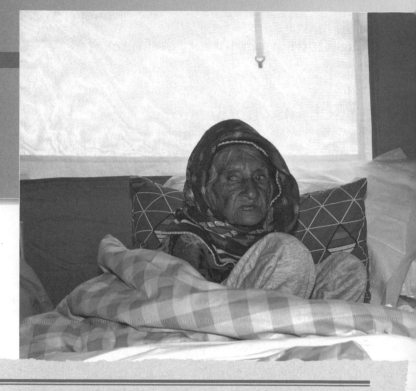

1. Read the story

Look at the pictures on these pages.
What is the story about? Now read it.

BAM, IRAN ¹For **over** a week, Shahr-Banu Mazandarani, 97, lay all alone under rubble* after an **earthquake** destroyed her home and her beautiful old town. ²The nights were long and cold, and the days were full of **fear**. ³Death was all around, but this **brave** woman, almost a **century** old, did not **give up**.

⁴Eight days after the earthquake, **rescuers** did not **expect** to find anyone still alive under the rubble. ⁵Then search dogs discovered Shahr-Banu. Rescuers heard a small voice, and they dug for three hours to **reach** her. ⁶Imagine their **excitement** when they pulled her out. The small woman was not only alive, she was unhurt! ⁷"Can I have some tea?" she asked soon **afterward**. ⁸People under earthquake rubble can usually live for only three days. But Shahr-Banu was lucky. When the earthquake hit, she was in bed, with many blankets **covering** her. "No one expected her to be alive," said an official. "It's a miracle**."

---

* rubble: broken stones from a damaged building
** miracle: a wonderful and surprising thing that you cannot explain

NEW WORDS

over *prep*	brave *adj*	rescuer *n*	excitement *n*
earthquake *n*	century *n*	expect *v*	afterward *adv*
fear *n*	give up *v*	reach *v*	cover *v*

>> See Glossary on page 93. >>

2. Rate the story

How much did you like it? Mark an ✗.

Not at All   A Lot

①   ②   ③   ④   ⑤

3. Check your comprehension

Put the sentences in the correct order. Number them 1–6.

a. ___ She lay for a week under the rubble.

b. ___ Rescuers began to dig to reach the woman.

c. ___ They pulled her out.

d. ___ Dogs discovered the woman.

e. ___ Shahr-Banu went to bed under many blankets.

f. ___ An earthquake destroyed her home.

4. Check your vocabulary

Complete the sentences with the New Words.

a. After an ear_ _ _ _ _ _ _ hit her home, Shahr-Banu did not give _ _.

b. This b_ _ _ _ woman was almost a cen_ _ _ _ old.

c. After search dogs discovered the woman, res_ _ _rs dug for three hours to re_ _ _ her.

d. The woman lived because blankets _ _ _ered her as she lay in bed.

5. Listen to the story track 22

Now listen to the story two or three times. Look at the pictures below as you listen.

6. Retell the story

Cover the story and look at the pictures above. Retell the story using the New Words.

7. Answer the questions

About the story...

a. How long was the old woman under the rubble?

b. Why did she live so long?

c. How can you explain the rescuers' excitement?

d. What words do you think describe the woman?

About you...

e. What do you know about earthquakes?

f. Do you know anyone who is brave? Describe him or her.

g. Do you think you are brave? Why or why not?

h. Have you ever had a hard time but not given up? What happened?

8. Learn word partnerships

Study the partnerships below. Complete the sentences so they are true for you.

EXPECT		
expect	to do something	***Rescuers did not expect to find anyone still alive.***
		I expect to finish school soon.
		I expect to visit Australia next month.
	someone to do something	*My sister expects me to cook dinner.*
		I expect you to clean up your mess.
		Our teacher expects students to be on time.

a. I expect _____ soon.

b. _____ always expects me _____.

c. I expect _____ to help me with _____.

9. Learn word groups

Complete the sentences so they are true for you. Use words from the pictures.

NATURAL DISASTERS

an earthquake   a tornado   a flood   a wildfire   an avalanche   a tidal wave

a. I have seen _____.

b. I have never seen _____.

c. There was _____ in my country last year.

10. Take a dictation track 23

Use your own paper to write the dictation. Check your answers on page 87.

11. Complete the story

Use the words from the box to complete the story.

expected	brave	rescuers	fear
over	reached	afterward	

WHAT A MIRACLE!

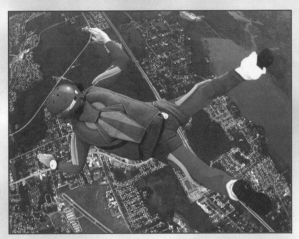

KUALA LUMPUR, MALAYSIA A woman has escaped death after she fell **(1)** _____ 1,500 meters.

Tan Lee Ping went skydiving* for the first time. When she jumped from the airplane, her skydiving teacher, Azlan Ismail, never **(2)** _____ her to have any trouble. He has been a teacher for 20 years and none of his students has ever had an accident.

But Ping did have trouble. Neither of her two parachutes** opened as she jumped. She was already unconscious*** when she **(3)** _____ the ground. **(4)** _____ took her to the hospital.

It was a miracle that Ping walked out of the hospital the same day! **(5)** _____, she said that as she fell she simply opened her arms as wide as possible. Ping seems to have no **(6)** _____. "I realize now that life is very short. From now on I'll just do what I can and try not to hesitate. I will jump again," the **(7)** _____ woman says.

_____

* skydiving: a sport where you jump from a plane
** parachutes: things like balloons that you use when you jump out of an airplane
*** unconscious: in a kind of sleep; not knowing what is happening

 Talk about the stories

Which story in this unit is the most surprising? Why? Which one did you like best? Why?

12

Boy Genius

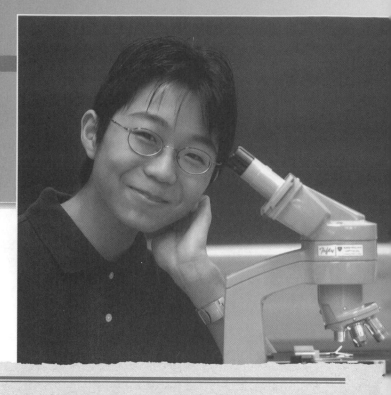

1. Read the story

Look at the pictures on these pages.
What is the story about? Now read it.

CHICAGO, USA ¹Sho Yano is a genius*. He is only 12, but he is already **studying medicine** at the University of Chicago! He wants to become a doctor. ²Sho enjoys school. "I love to learn," he says.

³Before Sho went to the university, he studied at home. His mother and father were his teachers because they could not find a school that was good **enough** for him. ⁴His mother taught him **math**. She had to study late into the night **in order to** keep **ahead** of her son. ⁵Sho can also play the **piano** beautifully, and he does tae kwon do.

⁶Sho **grew up** in California with his family. His mother is Korean, and his father is Japanese. ⁷He says that his parents never push him. "But sometimes I pull them along!" Sho smiles. His mother agrees with him. "He will decide his own life," she says. ⁸Sho **dreams of** fighting **diseases** like cancer** **in the future**. This **intelligent** young man will surely succeed!

---

* genius: a person who is very smart
** cancer: a very serious illness that makes some cells grow too fast

NEW WORDS

study *v*	math *n*	piano *n*	disease *n*
medicine *n*	in order to *conj*	grow up *v*	in the future *n*
enough *adv*	ahead *adv*	dream of *v*	intelligent *adj*

>> See Glossary on page 93. >>

2. Rate the story

How much did you like it? Mark an ✗.

Not at All   A Lot
① ② ③ ④ ⑤

3. Check your comprehension

Check (✔) the endings that are true.

a. Sho

___ is studying math at the university.

___ dreams of fighting cancer.

___ is intelligent.

___ can play the piano.

___ studied at home before he went to the university.

b. Sho's parents

___ were also his teachers.

___ are Japanese and Korean.

___ want to become doctors.

___ have to push Sho.

___ grew up in New York.

4. Check your vocabulary

Complete the sentences with the New Words.

a. Sho's mother taught him m_ _ _ herself because the schools were not good en_ _ _ _ for Sho.

b. She had to study hard in _ _ _ _ _ to keep ah_ _ _ of her son.

c. Sho d_ _ _ _ _ of fighting d_ _ _ _ _es like cancer.

d. He is an int_ _ _ _ _ _ _ _ young man!

5. Listen to the story track 24

Now listen to the story two or three times. Look at the pictures below as you listen.

6. Retell the story

Cover the story and look at the pictures above. Retell the story using the New Words.

7. Answer the questions

About the story…

a. What is unusual about Sho?

b. What does he do when he's not studying?

c. What do you know about his parents?

d. What questions would you like to ask Sho?

About you…

e. How are you like Sho? How are you different?

f. Where did you grow up? Who taught you?

g. How much do your parents push you?

h. What do you want to do in the future?

8. Learn word partnerships

Study the partnerships below. Complete the sentences so they are true for you.

DREAM OF		
dream of	doing something	**Sho dreams of fighting cancer in the future.**
		I dream of being a soccer player.
		He has dreamed of studying in London for years.
		Alan dreams of traveling the world.
	something	I'm dreaming of summer!
		She is dreaming of a new car.

a. I'm always dreaming of _____.

b. I have dreamed of _____ for many years.

c. My best friend dreams _____.

9. Learn word groups

Complete the sentences so they are true for you. Use words from the pictures.

SCHOOL SUBJECTS

math   music   chemistry   biology   geography   history

a. I enjoy studying _____.

b. I don't enjoy studying _____.

c. I think _____ is more difficult than _____.

10. Take a dictation track 25

Use your own paper to write the dictation. Check your answers on page 87.

11. Complete the story

Use the words from the box to complete the story.

in order to	intelligent	in the future
ahead	dreams of	enough	grew up

MOTHER SELLS HOME FOR SON'S FUTURE

CHESTER, ENGLAND   A woman has sold her home in Stockport **(1)** _____ send her son to ballet* school.

Until recently**, Eileen Morgan was living in a large, three-bedroom house. Her two sons **(2)** _____ there. Then one day, her 11-year-old son, James, who loves to dance, got lucky. The smart boy won a place at the Hammond School, one of the best ballet schools in England. Morgan was happy that her son could go to the school, but she was worried. It cost $74,000 for five years. How was she going to pay? She wasn't rich **(3)** _____!

So Morgan sold their comfortable house and everything in it. She moved her family into a small trailer***. "When you have a special child, you have to do everything to help them get **(4)** _____," she says. Her younger

son, Edward, is just as **(5)** _____ as James, and he also loves to dance. He **(6)** _____ following James to ballet school **(7)** _____.

---

  *ballet: a kind of dancing that tells a story with music but no words
 **recently: not long ago
***trailer: a small house on wheels that a car can pull

 Talk about the stories

How are Sho Yano's and James Morgan's families and lives similar? How are they different?

1. Match the words with the pictures.

___ **a.** insect
___ **b.** rescuer
___ **c.** math

___ **d.** medicine
___ **e.** wedding
___ **f.** piano

1.

2.

3.

4.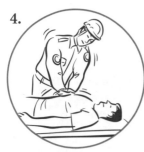

5.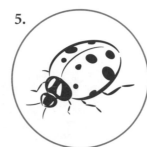

6.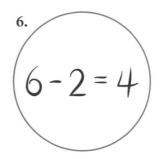

2. Write the words in the picture.

| grass | couple | blanket | neighbor | stereo | can |

3. Are the sentences true or false? Check (✔) the correct box.

		T	F
a.	Some diseases can spread from person to person.	☐	☐
b.	Music gets louder when you turn down a stereo.	☐	☐
c.	Some insects bite people.	☐	☐
d.	Soccer players run back and forth on the field.	☐	☐
e.	Earthquakes can destroy apartment buildings.	☐	☐
f.	We are now living in the twentieth century.	☐	☐

4. Circle the item that completes each sentence.

a. It was a beautiful, _____ afternoon.

   1. clean   2. calm   3. brave   4. wide

b. The child asked the question _____.

   1. over and over   2. ahead   3. back and forth   4. either

c. The blanket _____ the children and kept them warm.

   1. cleaned   2. fixed   3. covered   4. threw

d. The police _____ caught the criminal.

   1. rescuer   2. chief   3. couple   4. can

e. I _____ the couple on their new baby.

   1. congratulated   2. invited   3. discovered   4. picked up

f. The woman _____ for a minute before she made the difficult phone call.

   1. repaired   2. hesitated   3. bothered   4. reached

5. Match the words with the definitions.

a. be used to ___	1. thankful
b. afterward ___	2. in front of someone (or something)
c. grateful ___	3. able to think and learn quickly
d. brave ___	4. know something well because you have seen or done it a lot
e. ahead ___	5. later
f. intelligent ___	6. ready to do dangerous or difficult things without fear

6. Use the words from the box to complete the sentences.

joined	care	wide	destroy	kindness	math	give up
back and forth		enough	wedding	over	habit	

a. Singapore has _____ a movement that wants to spread _____ around the world.

b. Stephanie Boddy and her friend held their blanket open _____ and ran _____ as the little boy fell from the window.

c. The tornado did not _____ Jennifer Wells' _____ dress.

d. Paisit Chanta eats a worm a day and doesn't _____ what anyone thinks about his _____.

e. For _____ a week, Shahr-Banu Mazandarani lay under rubble after an earthquake destroyed her home, but she did not _____.

f. Sho Yano learned _____ from his mother because she could not find a school that was good _____ for him.

7. Use the words from the box to complete the story.

dig	as	reach	nearby	in order to
	rescuers	realized	apartment	

Man Spends Two Days Under Books

NEW YORK CITY, USA Patrice Moore, 43, spent forty-eight hours lying under a mountain of books and newspapers.

How did this happen? For ten years, Moore saved every single old paper. His **(1)** _____ was also full of books, and newspapers were several meters high on the floor. One day **(2)** _____ Moore was standing in his living room, everything fell down on him.

After two days, neighbors heard a strange noise and **(3)** _____ that Moore was in trouble. They went into the apartment and began to **(4)** _____ through the mountain of papers **(5)** _____ find Moore. Fire fighters soon joined the neighbors, and after a lot of work, the **(6)** _____ were able to

(7) _____ the man and pull him out. Moore went to a **(8)** _____ hospital and was grateful to be alive. "I didn't think I was going to get out," he said.

8. Check (✔) yes or no.

	Yes	No
a. I study very hard at school.	☐	☐
b. I have over 50 CDs.	☐	☐
c. I clean my room every day.	☐	☐
d. I am an excellent dancer.	☐	☐
e. I often invite a friend to have tea or coffee.	☐	☐
f. My friends don't have stereos, and I don't either.	☐	☐
g. Sometimes I throw cans in the street.	☐	☐
h. My eyes as well as my hair are brown.	☐	☐

9. Complete the sentences so they are true for you.

a. I listen to the music of _____ over and over.

b. I never share my _____ with anyone.

c. I am crazy about _____.

d. I eat healthy foods like _____ and _____.

e. My _____ was less expensive than my _____.

f. I grew up in _____.

g. Sometimes _____ bothers me because _____.

h. I like to invite _____ for _____.

i. I am proud of _____.

j. I always hang my _____ in the closet.

10. Fill in the chart with names of classmates. Try to write a different name in each blank. Walk around the room and ask questions such as:

Do you spend a lot of time outdoors?
Do you play the piano?

The winner is the first person to fill in seven blanks.

FIND SOMEONE WHO...

a. spends a lot of time outdoors. _____

b. plays the piano. _____

c. dreams of studying medicine in the future. _____

d. has a very clean room or apartment. _____

e. can fix a bike. _____

f. has felt an earthquake. _____

g. has a fear of insects. _____

h. expects to study English for many more years. _____

i. has pleasant neighbors. _____

j. likes excitement. _____

13

Fighting Crime with Books

1. Read the story

Look at the pictures on these pages.
What is the story about? Now read it.

MEXICO CITY, MEXICO [1]Like many big **cities**, Mexico City has a **problem** with crime in its subways*. [2]But it has found an unusual way to fight back—not with more police or bigger prisons but with books! The city is trying to make its **underground** stations big **libraries**. [3]Javier Gonzales Garza, the head of the subway, says, "when people read, people change."

[4]The city has given free books to subway riders **since** 2004 and wants to **give away** millions more in the future. [5]The city hopes that readers will **return** the books when they finish, but no one is checking. [6]The books **contain** very short stories, so people can read them during a quick subway ride. [7]Passengers love the idea. "The books just fly out of our hands," says one book volunteer**.

[8]The city is also putting **art** in some subway stations. Will books and art make the city **safer** and keep people out of prison? Not everyone is sure. "Maybe we'll just get more **educated** criminals," says one rider.

---

* subways: train systems that run under the ground
** volunteer: a person who does a job for no money

NEW WORDS

city *n*	underground *adj*	since *prep*	return *v*	art *n*	educated *adj*
problem *n*	library *n*	give away *v*	contain *v*	safe *adj*	

>> See Glossary on page 94. >>

2. Rate the story

How much did you like it? Mark an ✗.

Not at All   A Lot
①   ②   ③   ④   ⑤

3. Check your comprehension

Match the first and second parts of the sentences.

a. Mexico City is trying to fight ___

b. The city's subway stations are now also ___

c. The city will give away ___

d. The books contain ___

e. In some stations, you can also see ___

1. art.

2. millions of books.

3. libraries.

4. crime.

5. stories that are very short.

4. Check your vocabulary

Complete the sentences with the New Words.

a. S_ _ _ _ 2004, Mexico C_ _ _ has given _ _ _ _ many books in its subway stations.

b. It is also putting a_ _ in some underg_ _ _ _ _ stations.

c. Will the new lib_ _ _ies make the city s_ _er?

d. One rider said, "We'll just get more ed_ _ _ _ _ _ criminals."

5. Listen to the story track 26

Now listen to the story two or three times. Look at the pictures below as you listen.

6. Retell the story

Cover the story and look at the pictures above. Retell the story using the New Words.

7. Answer the questions

About the story...

a. Why is Mexico City giving away books in the subways?

b. What happens if readers do not return the books?

c. What do the books contain?

d. Do you think the city's plan will work? Why or why not?

About you...

e. How does your city fight crime?

f. What kind of books or stories do you like to read?

g. Who is the best-educated person that you know?

h. Has a book changed you or your ideas? How?

8. Learn word partnerships

Study the partnerships below. Complete the sentences so they are true for you.

PROBLEM	
have a problem with something	***Mexico City has a problem with crime.*** *I have a problem with my leg.* *She has a problem with her car.*
be a (big / serious / huge) problem	*Crime is a big problem in my town.* *Traffic is not a serious problem.* *Pollution is a huge problem.*

a. I have a problem _____.

b. _____ is a _____ problem in my city.

c. _____ is not a _____ problem here.

9. Learn word groups

Complete the sentences so they are true for you. Use words from the picture.

PLACES IN THE CITY

a. My city has _____ that is very beautiful.

b. We need _____.

c. There is _____ near my house, but there isn't _____.

10. Take a dictation track 27

Use your own paper to write the dictation. Check your answers on page 87.

11. Complete the story

Use the words from the box to complete the story.

library	city	contained	big problem	educated

BOOKS ARE HIS PUNISHMENT

YENIFAKILI, TURKEY A judge* in the Turkish **(1)** _____ of Yenifakili gave a criminal an unusual punishment**. The judge decided that he was not going to send the young man to prison. He had a better idea. The judge wanted Alparslan Yigit to become a more **(2)** _____ man.

He sent Yigit to the **(3)** _____ every day for a month. For 90 minutes a day, Yigit had to read books that **(4)** _____ news about the world or short stories. But Yigit did not like reading. He said that it was a **(5)** _____ for him and added, "It's like doing the dishes at home."

A police officer sat next to Yigit while he read. The officer had to check that the criminal was really reading, not just turning the pages.

---

* judge: a person who decides what to do with criminals
** punishment: a way of making someone suffer when they do something wrong

 Talk about the stories

How are the two stories in this unit similar? Do you think that books can make people nicer or more honest? Why or why not?

14

Back in the Water Again

1. Read the story

Look at the pictures on these pages.
What is the story about? Now read it.

HANALEI, HAWAII, USA [1]It was early morning and Bethany Hamilton, a star surfer*, was waiting for a **wave** off the **coast** of Hawaii. The water was **clear**, and the waves were **gentle**. [2]Bethany, 13, was lying on her surfboard** with her arms in the water. Suddenly, a shark*** **appeared** out of nowhere and bit off her left arm just below the **shoulder**. [3]"The water around me was red with blood," Bethany said later. She **remained** calm while her friends got her to the beach. Although she was **bleeding** heavily and in **pain**, she never cried.

[4]Bethany is one of the best young surfers in the USA. [5]Several weeks after she lost her arm, she was smiling on TV and telling her story. "I'm lucky," she said. "I'm alive!" [6]A month after the **attack**, Bethany returned to the water on her surfboard. [7]Friends on the beach cried when Bethany stood up on her board and rode her first wave. [8]"Man, she's **fantastic**," said a friend. "She gives people hope."

---

   * surfer: a person who rides on waves on a board
  ** surfboard: a long board that a surfer uses
*** shark: a big fish with sharp teeth that lives in the sea

NEW WORDS

wave *n*	**clear** *adj*	**appear** *v*	**remain** *v*	**pain** *n*	**fantastic** *adj*
coast *n*	**gentle** *adj*	**shoulder** *n*	**bleed** *v*	**attack** *n*	

>> See Glossary on page 94. >>

2. Rate the story

How much did you like it? Mark an ✗.

Not at All   A Lot

① ② ③ ④ ⑤

3. Check your comprehension

Check (✔) the endings that are true.

a. The shark bit off Bethany's

___ arm.

___ foot.

___ shoulder.

b. Just after the attack, Bethany was

___ calm.

___ in pain.

___ crying.

c. Several weeks later, she was

___ on TV.

___ back on her surfboard.

___ giving people hope.

4. Check your vocabulary

Complete the sentences with the New Words.

a. Bethany was waiting for a w_ _ _ in the clear waters off the co_ _ _ of Hawaii.

b. A shark ap_ _ _ _ed suddenly and bit off her arm below the sh_ _ _ _ _ _.

c. Bethany was bl_ _ _ing after the shark at_ _ _ _, but she rem_ _ _ed calm.

d. "She's fan_ _ _ _ _ _," said a friend.

5. Listen to the story 🔘 track 28

Now listen to the story two or three times. Look at the pictures below as you listen.

6. Retell the story

Cover the story and look at the pictures above. Retell the story using the New Words.

7. Answer the questions

About the story...

a. What happened to Bethany?

b. What did she do a month after the attack?

c. Why did friends cry when Bethany stood up on her board?

d. What words do you think describe Bethany?

About you...

e. What would you like to say to Bethany?

f. Have you ever been near a dangerous animal? Where?

g. What do you do at the beach?

h. Are you a calm person like Bethany? Why or why not?

8. Learn word partnerships

Study the partnerships below. Complete the sentences so they are true for you.

PAIN			

be in
    terrible / a lot of
    quite a bit of
	pain		**Bethany was in pain.**
			She was in terrible pain.
			The man was in quite a bit of pain.

not feel	any much	pain	*I didn't feel any pain when I broke my leg.* *She didn't feel much pain after the accident.*

a. _____ had an accident and _____ pain.

b. When I last went to the dentist, I _____ pain.

c. I _____ pain when I _____.

9. Learn word groups

Complete the sentences so they are true. Use words from the picture.

IN THE WATER

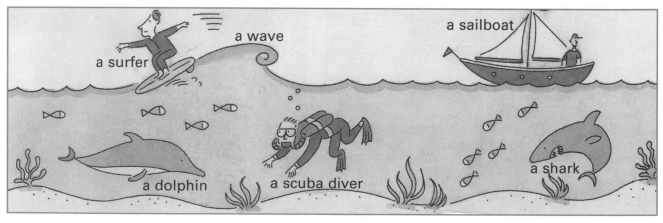

a. _____ is friendly to swimmers and surfers.

b. _____ loves big waves.

c. Scuba divers and surfers have to be careful of _____ attack.

10. Take a dictation ⊙ track 29

Use your own paper to write the dictation. Check your answers on page 87.

11. Complete the story

Use the words from the box to complete the story.

bleeding	**sailboat**	**remained**	**terrible pain**
attack	**clear**	**gentle**	

DOLPHINS SAVE TOURIST FROM SHARKS

EGYPT   Three British tourists were in a **(1)** _____ on the **(2)** _____ waters of the Red Sea. When they saw a group of dolphins* in the water, they decided to go swimming with them. Later, two of the men returned to the boat while the third man, Martin Richardson, **(3)** _____ in the water a bit longer.

Suddenly, the men on the boat heard a scream. When they looked at Richardson, they saw that the water all around him was red. "Dolphins are always **(4)** _____, so we knew that he was **(5)** _____ from a shark **(6)** _____," said one friend. They quickly took their boat to Richardson. Three dolphins were swimming in a circle around the man—jumping into the air and hitting the water with their tails**. They were keeping the sharks away!

Richardson was in **(7)** _____, but he was lucky. The dolphins saved him. Soon after the attack, he was resting comfortably in an Egyptian hospital. He did not lose an arm or a leg.

_____

* dolphins: intelligent animals that live in the sea
** tails: a tail is the long, thin part at the end of an animal's body

 Talk about the stories

How are the stories of Bethany Hamilton and Martin Richardson similar? How are they different?

15

Cows Prefer Beethoven

1. Read the story

Look at the pictures on these pages.
What is the story about? Now read it.

HEPHZIBAH, GA., USA ¹Mr. McElmurray, a **farmer**, had a problem. His 300 cows were not giving him **enough** milk. He often **complained** about it to his ten-year-old son, Daniel. ²The boy had an idea. "**Should** we play music for the cows?" he **wondered**. "**Perhaps** then they will give us more milk."

³So Daniel did an **experiment**. For a week he played loud rock music for the cows. But it did not help at all. ⁴The next week the cows listened to country music. They gave only a little **extra** milk. ⁵The third week Daniel played classical music*— Beethoven, Mozart, and Bach—for the cows. They gave much more milk than before—450 kilograms more! Classical music was clearly their favorite.

⁶Daniel **entered** a school competition** and won first place for his experiment. ⁷"I **guess** slower, quieter music helps cows **relax**," he said afterward. ⁸Daniel is proud that he was able to **solve** his father's problem. But now there is another problem on the **farm**. His father does not like classical music!

---

* classical music: music from 18th and 19th century Europe
** competition: a game or test that people try to win

NEW WORDS

farmer *n*	**complain** *v*	**wonder** *v*	**experiment** *n*	**enter** *v*	**relax** *v*	**farm** *n*
enough *det*	**should** *v*	**perhaps** *adv*	**extra** *adj*	**guess** *v*	**solve** *v*	

>> See Glossary on page 95. >>

2. Rate the story

How much did you like it? Mark an ✗.

Not at All   A Lot
① ---- ② ---- ③ ---- ④ ---- ⑤

3. Check your comprehension

Put the sentences in the correct order. Number them 1–6.

a. ___ Daniel entered a school competition.

b. ___ He played different kinds of music for the cows for three weeks.

c. ___ The experiment showed that the cows prefer classical music.

d. ___ Daniel's father complained that his cows were not giving enough milk.

e. ___ He won first place for his interesting experiment.

f. ___ Daniel decided to try to solve his father's problem.

4. Check your vocabulary

Complete the sentences with the New Words.

a. Daniel's father, a fa_ _ _ _, wasn't getting en_ _ _ _ milk from his cows.

b. He often com_ _ _ _ _ed about it, so Daniel decided to do an exper_ _ _ _ _.

c. "Per_ _ _ s music will help the cows give us ex_ _ _ milk," he thought.

d. He was proud that he could so_ _ _ the problem on the f_ _ _.

5. Listen to the story track 30

Now listen to the story two or three times. Look at the pictures below as you listen.

6. Retell the story

Cover the story and look at the pictures above. Retell the story using the New Words.

7. Answer the questions

About the story...

a. Why did Daniel do the experiment?

b. What did he learn about the cows? Does this surprise you?

c. What happened when Daniel entered the competition?

d. What do you think will happen on the farm in the future?

About you...

e. What is your favorite kind of music?

f. What kind of experiments have you done?

g. What competitions have you entered?

h. How do you help your family?

8. Learn word partnerships

Study the partnerships below. Complete the sentences so they are true for you.

COMPLAIN		
complain about something (to someone)		***Mr. McElmurray complained about his cows to Daniel.*** *John complains about his job to his coworkers.* *I like to complain about the weather.*
complain	constantly loudly	*My sister complains constantly about the noise.* *Mimi complained loudly about the food.*

a. I _____ constantly about _____.

b. Sometimes I complain _____ to _____.

c. _____ complained about _____ to me.

9. Learn word groups

Complete the sentences so they are true for you. Use words from the pictures.

WAYS TO RELAX

listen to
music

eat out

see a movie

take a nap

take a walk

play a game

a. On Sundays, I love to _____.

b. I don't often _____.

c. In the evening, I often _____.

10. Take a dictation track 31

Use your own paper to write the dictation. Check your answers on page 87.

11. Complete the story

Use the words from the box to complete the story.

| should | experiment | wondered |
| eat out | relax | guess | extra |

Diners Prefer Beethoven

LEICESTER, ENGLAND   Researchers* at the University of Leicester had an interesting question. "Will diners** spend more money if a restaurant plays music?" they **(1)** _____.

So they did an **(2)** _____ at a restaurant named Softley's. First, they played no music at all. Diners spent about $38.00 each. When the restaurant played rock music, diners spent a little more—about $40.00 each. When classical music was playing, diners spent a lot of **(3)** _____ money—more than $44.00 each!

"We found that people who **(4)** _____ prefer classical music," one researcher explained. "Mozart and Beethoven help them **(5)** _____ and feel richer, and they spend more money in a restaurant." Diners who heard classical music were buying more desserts*** and coffees.

"I **(6)** _____ in the future we **(7)** _____ be more careful about our music," said James Davis, the restaurant owner. "We'll play what the diners like."

---

   *researchers: people who study something carefully and do experiments to find out more about it
  **diners: people who are eating in a restaurant
***desserts: sweet things that you eat at the end of a meal

 Talk about the stories

Imagine that you and a partner are Daniel McElmurray and James Davis. You are meeting for the first time. Tell each other about the experiments and how they will change your lives.

16

A Cool Hotel

1. Read the story

Look at the pictures on these pages.
What is the story about? Now read it.

QUEBEC, CANADA **¹**Do you like very cold weather? Then maybe you would like to visit the **Ice** Hotel in Quebec—an **extraordinary** hotel made of snow and ice. **²**The rooms and all the **furniture** in them are ice. You sleep on an ice bed—in warm blankets, of course!—and sit in an ice **armchair**. **³**Even the flowers and newspapers in the room are **frozen**. Only the bathroom has **heat**. **⁴**You can watch a movie in the frozen theater or, if you are thirsty, have a warm drink at the ice **cafe** and listen to a **band**. **⁵**Sang-hee Ha **recently** visited the hotel from Seoul, Korea. "I have always seen this in my **dreams**," she said, "but the real thing is **unbelievable**!"

⁶The hotel is only open for one **season** each year. **⁷**Each winter, about 35 builders work for six weeks to put up wood and metal walls. Then they cover everything with snow and water, which quickly harden to ice. **⁸**In spring, this ice **palace** slowly **disappears** until nothing remains but a small lake.

NEW WORDS

ice *n*	armchair *n*	cafe *n*	dream *n*	palace *n*
extraordinary *adj*	frozen *adj*	band *n*	unbelievable *adj*	disappear *v*
furniture *n*	heat *n*	recently *adv*	season *n*	

>> See Glossary on page 95. >>

2. Rate the story

How much did you like it? Mark an ✗.

Not at All   A Lot
①   ②   ③   ④   ⑤

3. Check your comprehension

Match the first and second parts of the sentences.

a. The Ice Hotel is open ___   1. heat.

b. The furniture is ___   2. frozen beds.

c. Only the bathrooms have ___   3. in the spring.

d. In the cafe, you can ___   4. for only one season.

e. Visitors sleep on ___   5. made of ice.

f. The hotel disappears ___   6. listen to a band.

4. Check your vocabulary

Complete the sentences with the New Words.

a. The extra_ _ _ _ _ _ _ _ hotel in Quebec is made of snow and i_ _.

b. The beds and _ _ _chairs are fr_ _ _ _.

c. You can listen to a b_ _ _ at the ice _ _ _ _.

d. The pal_ _ _ slowly dis_ _ _ _ _ _s in the spring.

5. Listen to the story track 32

Now listen to the story two or three times. Look at the pictures below as you listen.

6. Retell the story

Cover the story and look at the pictures above. Retell the story using the New Words.

7. Answer the questions

About the story...

a. How is the Quebec hotel different from other hotels?

b. What can you do there?

c. How do the builders make it?

d. Would you like to stay in the ice palace? Why or why not?

About you...

e. Does your town have snow and ice in the winter? When does it disappear?

f. What is your favorite season? Why?

g. What dream did you have recently?

h. What interesting place have you visited recently?

8. Learn word partnerships

Study the partnerships below. Complete the sentences so they are true for you.

BAND		
listen to join play (something) in	a band	***You can listen to a band at the Ice Hotel.*** *Debra joined a band.* *Ichiro plays guitar in a band.*
a pop/rock a popular a favorite	band	*Do you like the pop band Love Psychedelico?* *The Beatles were a popular band in England.* *My favorite band is the Black Eyed Peas.*

a. _____ a very popular band in my country.

b. My favorite _____ band is _____.

c. You can listen _____ at _____ in my town.

d. _____ play(s) _____ band.

9. Learn word groups

Complete the sentences so they are true for you. Use words from the picture.

BEDROOM FURNITURE

a mirror a dresser a lamp a desk a bed an armchair

a. There's _____ in my bedroom.

b. There isn't _____ or _____ in the room.

c. I sleep on _____ and do my homework at _____.

10. Take a dictation ⊙ track 33

Use your own paper to write the dictation. Check your answers on page 87.

11. Complete the story

Use the words from the box to complete the story.

recently	**furniture**	**seasons**
extraordinary	**armchairs**	**lamps**

A High Hotel

MYSORE, INDIA   Would you like to sleep high up in a big tree in the jungle*?
A hotel near Mysore, India, has three tree houses—each 30 meters high. Visitors
live in the trees with singing birds, wild monkeys**, and other animals.

   The tree houses have very simple
(1) _____—two beds and two
(2) _____. There are also gas***
(3) _____. The bathroom has a toilet
and a cold shower. The food at the hotel is
wonderful. You eat everything on a banana leaf.

   When should you visit the hotel? The best
(4) _____ are fall and winter because
it rains a lot in spring and summer in the Indian
jungle. Annie Brown, an American tourist,
visited the hotel **(5)** _____. "It's an
(6) _____ place," she says. "But don't
go if you're afraid of high places!"

   * jungle: a thick forest in a hot part of the world
   ** monkeys: animals with long tails that can climb trees
   *** gas: something like air that you burn to get light

 Talk about the stories

Which hotel would you most like to visit—the Ice Hotel in Canada or the tree house hotel
in India? Why?

Small Woman Is Big Hero

1. Read the story

Look at the pictures on these pages.
What is the story about? Now read it.

JAPAN **¹**At just 1.50 meters tall, Junko Tabei is a small woman, but she is a big **hero**. **²**In 1975, she became the first woman to reach the top of Mount Everest. **³**It was almost **impossible**. There was an avalanche*, and Tabei sometimes had to climb on her hands and knees to reach her **goal**. **⁴**Now she is over 60 years old, but Tabei is still climbing three or four mountains a year.

⁵But the world's mountains are in **serious** trouble, she says. And the **reason**? More and more climbers are leaving **trash**—bottles, cans, and old shoes—**all over** the mountains. **⁶**Tabei, a **leader** in conservation**, is trying to change that. As the head of a Japanese conservation **program**, she teaches young people all over Asia to **care for** their mountains. **⁷**She takes groups of young people into the mountains to **get rid of** the trash and **plant** trees. Recently, students from Korea, Japan, and Taiwan climbed Snow Mountain in Taiwan with her.

⁸"Mountains teach me a lot of things," Tabei says. "They teach me how small **my own** problems are."

---

* avalanche: snow that falls quickly down a mountain
** conservation: taking care of the world's forests, lakes, and mountains

NEW WORDS

hero *n*	**serious** *adj*	**all over** *adv*	**care for** *v*	**my own** *det pron*
impossible *adj*	**reason** *n*	**leader** *n*	**get rid of** *v*	
goal *n*	**trash** *n*	**program** *n*	**plant** *v*	

>> See Glossary on page 96. >>

2. Rate the story

How much did you like it? Mark an **✗**.

Not at All   A Lot

① ② ③ ④ ⑤

3. Check your comprehension

Correct five mistakes in the story summary.

Junko Tabei is a large woman and a big hero. When she climbed Mount
Everest in 1975, it was easy for her to reach her goal. Today, Tabei still loves to
swim. She says that mountains teach her how small her own problems are.
Mountains are in trouble, she says, because climbers are leaving trees all over
them. Tabei, the leader of a conservation program, is teaching people all over
Asia to care for their lakes.

4. Check your vocabulary

Complete the sentences with the New Words.

a. Junko Tabei, a le_ _ _ _ in conservation, says that mountains are in ser_ _ _ _ trouble.

b. And the rea_ _ _? People leave tr_ _ _ behind as they climb.

c. Tabei shows young people how to _ _ _ _ for the mountains.

d. They pl_ _ _ trees and get _ _ _ of cans, bottles, and old shoes.

5. Listen to the story   ⊙ track 34

Now listen to the story two or three times. Look at the pictures below as you listen.

6. Retell the story

Cover the story and look at the pictures above. Retell the story using the New Words.

7. Answer the questions

About the story…

a. What was Tabei's goal in 1975?

b. What is Tabei doing now?

c. Why does she like to be in the mountains?

d. Would you like to climb with her? Why or why not?

About you…

e. What can you do to help the mountains, lakes, or parks near you?

f. What do you do when you go to the mountains?

g. Would you like to climb Mount Everest? Why or why not?

h. Who are your heroes?

8. Learn word partnerships

Study the partnerships below. Complete the sentences so they are true for you.

GOAL		
reach achieve	a goal	**Tabei climbed on her hands and knees to reach her goal.** *John is sure that he will achieve his goals.* *I want to achieve my goal before I am 30.*
My goal is to do something		*My goal is to become a doctor.* *My goal is to have a restaurant in the future.*

a. One of my goals is to _____.

b. I want to _____ my goal before I am _____.

c. My best friend's goal is _____ in the future.

9. Learn word groups

Complete the sentences so they are true for you. Use words from the picture.

TRASH

a computer · a glass bottle · a soda can · a plastic bottle · paper · a cardboard box

a. In my trash can, you can find _____ and _____.

b. Sometimes I see a person throwing _____ on the street.

c. This week I picked up _____ off the street.

10. Take a dictation 🔘 track 35

Use your own paper to write the dictation. Check your answers on page 87.

11. Complete the story

Use the words from the box to complete the story.

impossible	hero	goal	serious	leader	program

Small Boy Is Big Hero

OTTAWA, CANADA When he was six years old, Ryan Hreljac, a Canadian, was already a **(1)** _____ to many people in Africa. How did this happen? Ryan's story began in 1998. His teacher told the six-year-old boy and his class* that many people in Africa were dying because they had no clean water. Ryan could not stop thinking about this **(2)** _____ problem. He told everyone about it, and then he and his family began to collect** money. Their **(3)** _____ was to build a water well*** in Africa.

Ryan collected enough money and built the well, but he did not stop there. He spoke to schoolchildren, collected more money, and built even more wells. About 150,000 more people in Africa now have clean water.

These days Ryan is a serious student with a lot of schoolwork. But in his free time he travels around the world to collect more money for his **(4)** _____—Ryan's Well Foundation.

Ryan is a true **(5)** _____ who tells children that they can change the world. "Nothing is **(6)** _____," he says. "Anyone can do anything. It doesn't matter who you are."

* class: a group of children who learn together
** collect: take things from different people and put them together
*** well: a deep hole for getting water from under the ground

 Talk about the stories

Imagine that you and a partner are Junko Tabei and Ryan Hreljac. You are meeting for the first time. Tell each other about your lives.

18

The Smartest Home

1. Read the story

Look at the pictures on these pages.
What is the story about? Now read it.

MEDINA, WASH., USA ¹Bill Gates, one of the world's richest people, lives near Seattle in the world's "smartest" home. More than 100 computers **control** everything in this fantastic mansion*.

²As Gates is driving home, he can **fill** his bath with water at the perfect **temperature**. ³When he gets near the **entrance**, the big **gate** opens just before his **arrival**. ⁴Sensors** under the floor follow his steps inside the house. When Gates **enters** a room, the lights turn on by themselves. He doesn't need to turn them off because they darken **automatically** as he leaves. ⁵His favorite music plays in each room as he walks through the house, and it can even follow him outside. ⁶When he jumps into the **pool** for a swim, the same music plays underwater. ⁷Gates has a lot of art on his walls, but he never gets tired of it. The pictures change automatically because they are digital***.

⁸A "smart home" is expensive now, but we can all **look forward to** living in **one** in the future. "It's going to happen very quickly," **promises** Dave Farber of the University of Pennsylvania.

---

  * mansion: a very large house
 ** sensors: small machines that can find movement
*** digital: stored as electronic signals

NEW WORDS

control *v*	temperature *n*	gate *n*	enter *v*	pool *n*	one *pron*
fill *v*	entrance *n*	arrival *n*	automatically *adv*	look forward to *v*	promise *v*

>> See Glossary on page 96. >>

2. Rate the story

How much did you like it? Mark an ✗.

Not at All   A Lot

  ①   ②   ③   ④   ⑤

3. Check your comprehension

Check (✔) the endings that are true.

a. Bill Gates

___ lives in New York.

___ is very rich.

___ has many computers in his home.

___ can fill his bath while in the car.

___ lives in a mansion.

b. His house has

___ a large gate.

___ sensors under the floors.

___ automatic doors.

___ digital art on the floors.

___ a pool.

4. Check your vocabulary

Complete the sentences with the New Words.

a. When Bill Gates is in his car, he can f_ _ _ his bath with water and con_ _ _ _ the temperature.

b. When he gets near the entrance to his house, the g_ _ _ opens just before his arr_ _ _ _.

c. When Gates en_ _ _ s his swimming p_ _ _, music plays underwater.

d. Dave Farber pr_ _ _ _ _s that we will all live in a smart house soon.

5. Listen to the story   track 36

Now listen to the story two or three times. Look at the pictures below as you listen.

6. Retell the story

Cover the story and look at the pictures above. Retell the story using the New Words.

7. Answer the questions

About the story...

a. What controls Gates' smart house?
b. What happens as Gates walks around his house?
c. How is Gates' house different from yours?
d. In your opinion, what is the best thing about Gates' house?

About you...

e. Would you like to live in a smart house? Why or why not?
f. What other things do you know about Bill Gates?
g. What extraordinary changes do you think we will see in the future?
h. Are you looking forward to them? Why or why not?

8. Learn word partnerships

Study the partnerships below. Complete the sentences so they are true for you.

LOOK FORWARD TO		
look forward to	doing something	***We can all look forward to living in a smart house.*** *I look forward to meeting you.* *I'm looking forward to starting college next year.*
	something	*She's looking forward to her trip.* *We're really looking forward to the party!* *I always look forward to the weekend.*

a. I always look forward to going _____.
b. I _____ looking forward to _____ next weekend.
c. I'm not looking forward _____.

9. Learn word groups

Complete the sentences so they are true for you. Use words from the picture.

A MANSION

a driveway
a garage
a pool
a tennis court
a lawn
a gate

a. My house or apartment has _____ but doesn't have _____.
b. I would like to have _____.
c. I don't need _____.

10. Take a dictation track 37

Use your own paper to write the dictation. Check your answers on page 87.

11. Complete the story

Use the words from the box to complete the story.

arrival	controls	entrance	temperature
garage	automatically	lawn	

A FUN HOME

PALOS HILLS, ILL., USA   Ben Skora, 69, is an extraordinary inventor*. He has built himself a "house of the future." Although the house is not large, it is fantastic. Everything in it works by itself—the doors, the toilets, the music, the room **(1)** _____, and the furniture. Skora **(2)** _____ everything with his cell phone. "I can work everything in the house even when I'm in Tokyo," he says.

On your **(3)** _____ the first fantastic thing you see is the **(4)** _____ to Skora's house. It looks like something from the next century. A small, round door opens **(5)** _____, and a talking robot**, Arok, is there to say hello and bring you a drink.

Skora can move his walls with his cell phone. His chairs can speed around the room. In the bathroom, an arm comes out of the wall to give you soap***.

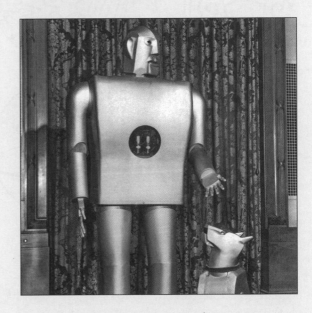

Arok the robot cleans Skora's carpet and waters his **(6)** _____.

Skora builds everything in his **(7)** _____. People say that he is a genius. "But my family," says Skora, "thinks I'm crazy."

---

* inventor: a person who makes or thinks of something new
** robot: a machine that can work like a person
*** soap: something that you use with water for washing

 ## Talk about the stories

How are the houses of Bill Gates and Ben Skora similar? How are they different? Which one would you like to live in? Why?

1. Match the words with the pictures.

_____ **a.** wave

_____ **b.** palace

_____ **c.** pain

_____ **d.** entrance

_____ **e.** trash

_____ **f.** furniture

_____ **g.** shoulder

_____ **h.** farmer

1.
2.
3.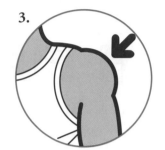
4.

5.
6.
7.
8.

2. Write the words in the picture.

| cafe | ice | armchair | band | pool | gate | art |

3. Are the sentences true or false? Check (✔) the correct box.

		T	F
a.	Spring and summer are seasons.	☐	☐
b.	Computers control many things.	☐	☐
c.	New York City is on the Pacific Coast.	☐	☐
d.	A library contains books.	☐	☐
e.	The sun appears at night and disappears in the morning.	☐	☐
f.	An armchair is a piece of furniture.	☐	☐

4. Circle the item that completes each sentence.

a. I'm using Hideaki's bike today and plan to _____ it tomorrow.

   1. remain   2. return   3. promise   4. enter

b. The _____ of the palace is very beautiful.

   1. entrance   2. arrival   3. coast   4. underground

c. There is no _____ in the building; it's so cold!

   1. ice   2. pain   3. heat   4. temperature

d. Sam's _____ is to go to college.

   1. goal   2. hero   3. attack   4. gate

e. My trip to the Great Wall of China was _____!

   1. extra   2. heat   3. clear   4. extraordinary

5. Match the words with the definitions.

a. unbelievable ____   1. to make things or people do what you want

b. wonder ____   2. everywhere

c. guess ____   3. very cold, like ice

d. control ____   4. very surprising or unusual

e. all over ____   5. to give an answer when you do not know if it is right

f. frozen ____   6. to ask yourself something

6. Use the words from the box to complete the sentences.

fill	given away	bleeding	entered	extraordinary	attack
own	leader	arrival	extra	frozen	since

a. Mexico City has _____ free books _____ 2004.

b. Bethany was _____ heavily after the shark _____.

c. Daniel McElmurray _____ a school competition and showed how he got _____ milk from his father's cows.

d. The Ice Hotel in Canada is an _____ hotel with _____ furniture.

e. Junko Tabei, a _____ in conservation, says, "Mountains teach me how small my _____ problems are."

f. Bill Gates can _____ his bathtub before his _____.

7. Use the words from the box to complete the story.

program	reason	enough	library
one	safe	extraordinary	

Student Lives in Library

NEW YORK CITY, USA A New York student slept in a college library for eight months.

The **(1)** _____? Steve Stanzak, 20, did not have **(2)** _____ money to pay for both college and an apartment. College is very expensive, he said, and he was not getting any help from his parents.

"It was quite comfortable," Stanzak said later. He slept in a small room, washed himself in the **(3)** _____ bathroom, and always felt **(4)** _____. Stanzak is a good student who studies in the writing **(5)** _____ at New York University.

Officials at the university were surprised. "It's **(6)** _____," said **(7)** _____. The university has decided to give Stanzak a free apartment for the rest of the year.

8. Check (✔) *yes* or *no*.

	Yes	No
a. I often complain about the temperature.	☐	☐
b. I cared for a child recently.	☐	☐
c. My dream is to become rich.	☐	☐
d. I like to swim in big waves.	☐	☐
e. I feel safe in my city.	☐	☐
f. I like to solve serious problems.	☐	☐
g. I live on a farm.	☐	☐
h. I relax in front of the TV most evenings.	☐	☐
i. I usually remember my dreams.	☐	☐
j. I would like to live in a palace.	☐	☐

9. Complete the sentences so they are true for you.

a. I think _____ is fantastic!

b. Perhaps I should get rid of my _____ and buy a new one.

c. My hero is _____.

d. My favorite band is _____.

e. I was in a lot of pain when _____.

f. It is impossible for me to _____.

g. I look forward to _____ in the future.

h. I think _____ is a very gentle person.

10. Fill in the chart with names of classmates. Try to write a different name in each blank. Walk around the room and ask questions such as:

Would you like to live on a farm?
Do you like art?

The winner is the first person to fill in seven blanks.

FIND SOMEONE WHO...

a. would like to live on a farm. _____

b. likes art. _____

c. often plants flowers. _____

d. is in a band or wants to be. _____

e. likes to relax in cafes. _____

f. gives away old clothes. _____

g. wants to become a world leader. _____

h. loves cold temperatures. _____

i. likes to do experiments. _____

j. wants to become very educated. _____

Dictations

Unit 1

Airport officials searched the Canadian woman carefully. When they didn't find any coins or metal on her, they let her board the plane. Later, the woman got an X-ray. She was surprised when she learned about the instrument in her stomach. "No one is perfect," explained a hospital official.

Unit 2

Sokolov is responsible for taking care of some homes in the winter. His job can be extremely dangerous. He wanted to scare criminals, so he put on large boots and walked in the snow all around his neighborhood. Clearly, the boots have worked!

Unit 3

Mr. Magon didn't like the wild pink hair of his students at all. He wanted to bring order to the school, so he sent a letter to the parents. The parents discussed the principal's idea. Then they warned him that they would take him to court. Magon was very surprised.

Unit 4

Shi-tung is a college student who plays a lot of online computer games. Although the games are fun to play, he says it's a bit hard to stop. His parents don't mind that he spends so much time on the computer, so his hobby does not lead to family fights.

Unit 5

Mike Hill got stuck in the mud while he was hunting. He was not able to move. Fire fighters tried to save him, but they became stuck, too. A helicopter finally pulled everyone up, one by one. The pilot said that it was a terrible mess.

Unit 6

Some police officers in France have a cool job. They skate four hours a day through the lovely streets of Paris. They chase thieves and try to catch up with them. They have to stay in shape, so they go to the gym. Tourists love the cops on wheels!

Unit 7

Singapore wants to spread kindness and make the world more pleasant. Here are three of their ideas: Try not to bother your neighbors with loud music. Turn down your stereo at night. Share your lunch with a new student at school. And don't forget to smile!

Unit 8

It was a calm afternoon. The girls were sitting on the grass outdoors and looking up at the clouds. When they saw the small boy falling, they ran to catch him. The boy turned over and over as he fell, and the girls moved back and forth with their blanket.

Unit 9

While the couple were repairing and cleaning their house, they hung the wedding dress in a workshop nearby. A tornado destroyed the house as well as the trees but not the workshop. Dan was happy when he discovered the dress, untouched. The bride and groom cried at their wedding.

Unit 10

Would you like to eat a scorpion, a fly, or a spider? Chanta has a habit of eating a worm a day! He is crazy about worms. He thinks they are like medicine and keep you healthy. Chanta's coworkers are used to his habit but still think it's strange. Chanta doesn't care what others think!

Unit 11

When the earthquake hit, the brave woman was in bed. Many blankets covered her and kept her alive for over a week. When rescuers reached her, there was so much excitement! They did not expect her to be alive. Soon afterward, the woman asked for tea.

Unit 12

Sho is only 12, but he is already studying at the university. Medicine and biology are two of his school subjects. This intelligent boy dreams of becoming a doctor in order to fight diseases like cancer. Sho loves school, but he also plays sports and the piano.

Unit 13

Crime is a huge problem in many cities. Mexico City wants to make its subways safer. Since 2004, the city has given away many free books and has put art in the stations. The passengers love the new underground libraries! The city thinks that educated people will stay away from crime.

Unit 14

The attack happened suddenly. Bethany was lying on her surfboard with her arms in the water. The water was clear and gentle. Then the shark appeared out of nowhere and bit her arm. Bethany remained calm although she was in terrible pain. Her friends say that she is fantastic.

Unit 15

Daniel's father, a farmer, had a problem with his cows. He often complained about it to Daniel. The boy solved the problem. He did an experiment and showed that cows like classical music. It helps them relax, and so they give a lot of extra milk.

Unit 16

The beds, dressers, and armchairs in the Ice Hotel are all frozen. A visitor from Korea said it was unbelievable. She said that she saw the extraordinary hotel in her dreams. The palace is only open for the winter season. It disappears in the spring.

Unit 17

Junko Tabei loves mountains. The reason, she says, is that they teach her many things. As a leader in conservation, she teaches people to care for them. She plants trees in the mountains and gets rid of trash like soda cans and plastic bottles. Her goal is to keep mountains clean.

Unit 18

Bill Gates controls everything in his house with computers. Before his arrival home, the gate to his driveway opens. He can also fill his bath to a perfect temperature. Would you like to live in a smart house? We can all look forward to having one in the future.

Glossary

Unit 1

metal *n* gold and silver are examples of metals

official *n* a person who does important work

check *v* to look at someone or something to see that it is right or good

coin *n* a round piece of money that is made of metal

search *v* to look carefully to find something

let *v* to allow someone to do something

pass *v* to go past someone or something

board *v* to get on a plane, ship, bus, or train

several *adj* more than two, but not many

stomachache *n* when your stomach hurts

instrument *n* a thing that you use for doing a special job

operation *n* cutting open a person's body to take out or fix a part inside

surprised *adj* feeling or showing surprise

perfect *adj* very good, with nothing wrong

Unit 2

guard *n* a person who keeps someone or something out of danger

take care of *v* to look after someone or something; do what is necessary

owner *n* a person who has something—for example, a home owner or a car owner

be responsible for *v* to be the person who must do something

plenty of *n* a lot

neighborhood *n* a part of a town

idea *n* a thought or plan in your head

extremely *adv* very

boot *n* a heavy shoe that comes above your ankle

step *n* when you move your foot up and put it down in another place, you take a step

clearly *adv* without a doubt; certainly

study *v* to look at something carefully

almost *adv* nearly

scare *v* to make someone afraid

Unit 3

knee *n* the part of a pant leg that covers your knee; the part in the middle of your leg that bends

pink *adj* with a light red color

principal *n* a person who is the head of a school

not at all *adv* not even a little

uniform *n* the special clothes that everyone in the same job or school wears

order *n* when everyone is doing the right thing or everything is in the right place

parent *n* a mother or father

punish *v* to make someone suffer when they do something wrong

suitably *adv* in the right or correct way

discuss *v* to talk about something

warn *v* to tell someone about danger or about something bad that will happen

court *n* a place where people decide if a person did something wrong

argue *v* to talk angrily with someone because you do not agree

Unit 4

hobby *n* something that you like doing when you are not working

game *n* something that you play that has rules

college *n* a place where people go to learn after high school

mind *v* to feel unhappy or angry about something

each other *pron* words that show that someone does the same thing as another person

university *n* a place where people go to learn after high school. It is like a college, but you can go for longer than four years.

lead to *v* to make something happen

add *v* to say something more

although *conj* but

a bit *mod* a little

crazy *adj* wild

fun *n* something that you really enjoy

succeed *v* to get what you want

Unit 5

hunt *v* to look for and kill animals as a sport

lake *n* a body of water that is smaller than a sea

mud *n* soft, wet dirt

become *v* to change and begin to be something different

scared *adj* afraid

save *v* to take someone or something away from danger

success *n* doing well or getting what you want

engine *n* a machine that makes something move

be able to *v* can; to have the power to do something

helicopter *n* a kind of small airplane that can go straight up and down in the sky

safely *adv* without danger

one by one *adv* first one and then the next

basket *n* a container that you use to carry or hold things

mess *n* something dirty or a big problem

pilot *n* a person who flies an airplane or a helicopter

Unit 6

cool (informal) *adj* great

in-line skate *n* a shoe with wheels in a line on the bottom

lovely *adj* beautiful or very nice

police officer *n* a policeman or policewoman

speed *v* to go or move very fast

look out *v* to be careful

chase *v* to run behind someone and try to catch them

catch up with *v* to move quickly so that you are not behind someone

skate *v* to move on skates

in shape *adv* in good health

flat *adj* smooth; with no part higher or lower than the rest

seriously *adv* very badly

tourist *n* a person who visits a place on vacation

Unit 7

less *adv* not as much

join *v* to become part of a group

kindness *n* being nice and good to people

spread *v* to move to other places

pleasant *adj* nice, enjoyable, or friendly

excellent *adj* very good

bother *v* to do something that other people don't like

neighbor *n* a person who lives near you

turn down *v* to make a stereo, a TV, etc., quieter

stereo *n* a machine for playing CDs (or cassettes)

invite *v* to ask someone to come to something like a party, dinner, or movie

share *v* to give part of something you have to other people

throw *v* to move your arm to send something through the air

pick up *v* to take and lift something

Unit 8

congratulate *v* to tell someone that you are happy about something they have done

calm *adj* quiet; without much wind

outdoors *adv* outside, not in a building

grass *n* a plant with thin green leaves that covers fields and lawns

apartment *n* a group of rooms that you live in, in a larger building

blanket *n* something that keeps you warm in a bed

hesitate *v* to stop for a short time before you do something because you are not sure about it

as *conj* while; at the same time

over and over *adv* many times

wide *adv* as far or as much as possible

back and forth *adv* first one way and then the other, many times

be proud of *v* to be pleased about something that you or others have done

chief *n* a person who is at the head of a group

Unit 9

wedding *n* a time when a man and woman get married

repair *v* to make something that is broken good again; to fix

fix *v* to make something that is broken good again; to repair

clean *v* to take away the dirt from something

nearby *adv* not far away

hang *v* to attach from above

clean *adj* not dirty

as well as *conj* and also

destroy *v* to break something completely

discover *v* to find

couple *n* two people who are married

grateful *adj* thankful

Unit 10

insect *n* a very small animal that has six legs, like a fly

habit *n* something that you do very often

bite *v* to cut something with teeth

can *n* a metal container for food or drink

realize *v* to understand or know something

either *adv* (used in sentences with *not*) also

be crazy about *v* to like something very much

medicine *n* pills or special drinks that help you get better when you are sick

healthy *adj* well; not sick

dig *v* to move dirt and make a hole in the ground

be used to *v* to know something well because you have seen or done it a lot

care *v* to think that something is important

Unit 11

over *prep* more than

earthquake *n* a sudden, strong shaking of the ground

fear *n* the feeling that you have when you are afraid

brave *adj* ready to do dangerous or difficult things without fear

century *n* one hundred years

give up *v* to stop trying

rescuer *n* a person who saves someone from danger

expect *v* to think that something will happen

reach *v* to arrive somewhere

excitement *n* the feeling of being excited

afterward *adv* later

cover *v* to be over or on top of something

Unit 12

study *v* to spend time learning about something

medicine *n* the science that tries to understand illness and make sick people well again

enough *adv* as much as you need

math *n* the study of numbers

in order to *conj* so that you can do something

ahead *adv* in front of someone or something

piano *n* a big musical instrument that you play by hitting black and white keys

grow up *v* to change from a child to an adult

dream of *v* to hope for something nice

disease *n* an illness

in the future *n* in the time that will come

intelligent *adj* able to think and learn quickly

Unit 13

city *n* a big, important town

problem *n* something difficult that worries you

underground *adj* under the ground

library *n* a building where you go to borrow or read books

since *prep* in all the time after

give away *v* to give something to someone without getting money for it

return *v* to give, put, or take something back

contain *v* to have something inside it

art *n* beautiful things like paintings or drawings that someone has made

safe *adj* not in danger; not hurt

educated *adj* knowing a lot or having studied in a good school for many years

Unit 14

wave *n* one of the lines of water that moves across the top of the sea

coast *n* the part of the land that is next to the sea

clear *adj* easy to see through

gentle *adj* quiet; calm, not rough

appear *v* to come and be seen

shoulder *n* the part of your body between your neck and arm

remain *v* to stay the same way; to not change

bleed *v* to lose blood

pain *n* the feeling that you have in your body when you are hurt or sick

attack *n* trying to hurt someone

fantastic *adj* very good; wonderful

Unit 15

farmer *n* a person who takes care of a farm

enough *det* as much as you need

complain *v* to say that you do not like something

should *v* a word that you use to ask or tell someone what is the right thing to do

wonder *v* to ask yourself something

perhaps *adv* maybe

experiment *n* something you do to find out what will happen

extra *adj* more than what is usual

enter *v* to give your name to someone because you want to do something like take a test or be in a competition

guess *v* to give an answer when you do not know if it is right

relax *v* to be calm; to rest

solve *v* to find the answer to a problem

farm *n* land and buildings where people keep animals and grow food

Unit 16

ice *n* water that is hard because it is very cold

extraordinary *adj* very unusual or strange

furniture *n* tables, chairs, beds, etc.

armchair *n* a big, soft chair with arms

frozen *adj* very cold, like ice; something that is frozen cannot move

heat *n* something that makes a place warm

cafe *n* a place where you can have a drink and something small to eat

band *n* a group of people who play music together

recently *adv* not long ago

dream *n* the pictures or ideas in your head while you sleep

unbelievable *adj* very surprising or unusual

season *n* a part of the year like summer or winter

palace *n* a very large house where an important person lives

disappear *v* if something disappears, it goes away so that people cannot see it

Unit 17

hero *n* a person who has done something brave or good

impossible *adj* if something is impossible, you cannot do it

goal *n* something important that you hope to do in the future

serious *adj* very bad

reason *n* why something happens

trash *n* things that nobody wants

all over *adv* everywhere

leader *n* a person who is at the head of a group

program *n* a plan of things to do

care for *v* to do what is necessary for something or someone

get rid of *v* to take something away

plant *v* to put flowers, trees, etc., in the ground to grow

my own *det pron* belonging to me

Unit 18

control *v* to make things or people do what you want

fill *v* to make something full

temperature *n* how hot or cold something is

entrance *n* where you go into a place

gate *n* a kind of door in an outside wall

arrival *n* coming to a place

enter *v* to go into a place

automatically *adv* if something works automatically, it works by itself

pool *n* a place for swimming

look forward to *v* to feel happy or excited about something that is going to happen

one *pron* word that you use instead of the name of a person or thing

promise *v* to say that something will certainly happen

Index

A

a bit *mod* 14, 17, 65
add *v* 14, 17, 34, 61
afterward *adv* 46, 49, 66
ahead *adv* 50, 53
all over *adv* 74
almost *adv* 6, 17, 38, 46, 74
although *conj* 14, 17, 62, 81
apartment *n* 34
appear *v* 62
argue *v* 10
armchair *n* 70, 73
arrival *n* 78, 81
art *n* 58, 78
as *conj* 34, 37, 41, 49, 78
as well as *conj* 38
attack *n* 62, 65
automatically *adv* 78, 81

B

back and forth *adv* 34, 37
band *n* 70
basket *n* 18
be able to *v* 18, 21, 66
be crazy about *v* 42, 45
be proud of *v* 34, 37
be responsible for *v* 6, 9
be used to *v* 42
become *v* 18, 21, 25, 30, 50, 61, 74
bite *v* 42
blanket *n* 34, 46, 70
bleed *v* 62, 65
board *v* 2
boot *n* 6, 18
bother *v* 30, 33
brave *adj* 46, 49

C

cafe *n* 70
calm *adj* 34, 62
can *n* 42, 74
care *v* 42
care for *v* 74
catch up with *v* 22
century *n* 46, 81
chase *v* 22, 45
check *v* 2, 5, 17, 58, 61
chief *n* 34
city *n* 58, 61
clean *adj* 38, 77
clean *v* 38, 81
clear *adj* 62, 65
clearly *adv* 6, 9, 66
coast *n* 62
coin *n* 2
college *n* 14
complain *v* 66
congratulate *v* 34
contain *v* 58, 61
control *v* 78, 81
cool (informal) *adj* 22, 25
couple *n* 38, 41
court *n* 10
cover *v* 46, 70
crazy *adj* 14, 81

D

destroy *v* 38, 46
dig *v* 42, 45
disappear *v* 70
discover *v* 38, 41, 46
discuss *v* 10, 13
disease *n* 50
dream *n* 70
dream of *v* 50, 53

E

each other *pron* 14, 17
earthquake *n* 46
educated *adj* 58, 61
either *adv* 42
engine *n* 18
enough *adv* 50, 53
enough *det* 66, 77
enter [competition] *v* 66
enter [go into] *v* 78
entrance *n* 78, 81
excellent *adj* 30
excitement *n* 46
expect *v* 46, 49
experiment *n* 66, 69
extra *adj* 66, 69
extraordinary *adj* 70, 73, 81
extremely *adv* 6, 9

F

fantastic *adj* 62, 78, 81
farm *n* 66
farmer *n* 66
fear *n* 46, 49
fill *v* 78
fix *v* 38
flat *adj* 22
frozen *adj* 70
fun *n* 14, 17
furniture *n* 70, 73, 81

G

game *n* 14, 17
gate *n* 78
gentle *adj* 62, 65
get rid of *v* 74
give away *v* 58

give up *v* 46
goal *n* 74, 77
grass *n* 34, 37
grateful *adj* 38
grow up *v* 50, 53
guard *n* 6, 9, 37
guess *v* 66, 69

H

habit *n* 42, 45
hang *v* 38
healthy *adj* 42, 45
heat *n* 70
helicopter *n* 18
hero *n* 74, 77
hesitate *v* 34, 49
hobby *n* 14
hunt *v* 18

I

ice *n* 70
idea *n* 6, 9, 22, 25, 58, 61, 66
impossible *adj* 74, 77
in order to *conj* 50, 53
in shape *adv* 22, 25
in the future *n* 50, 53, 58, 69, 78
in-line skate *n* 22
insect *n* 42, 45
instrument *n* 2
intelligent *adj* 50, 53
invite *v* 30

J

join *v* 30

K

kindness *n* 30, 33
knee *n* 10, 13, 74

L

lake *n* 18, 21, 70
lead to *v* 14, 17
leader *n* 74, 77
less *adv* 30
let *v* 2, 5
library *n* 58, 61
look forward to *v* 78
look out *v* 22, 25
lovely *adj* 22

M

math *n* 50
medicine [pills and special drinks] *n* 42
medicine [subject] *n* 50
mess *n* 18, 21
metal *n* 2, 5, 70
mind *v* 14, 41
mud *n* 18, 21
my own *det pron* 74

N

nearby *adv* 38, 41
neighbor *n* 30, 33, 38
neighborhood *n* 6, 38, 45
not at all *adv* 10

O

official *n* 2, 5, 46
one *pron* 78
one by one *adv* 18, 42

operation *n* 2, 5
order *n* 10
outdoors *adv* 34, 37
over *prep* 46, 49, 74
over and over *adv* 34
owner *n* 6, 69

P

pain *n* 62, 65
palace *n* 70
parent *n* 10, 13, 14, 30, 50
pass *v* 2
perfect *adj* 2, 13, 25
perhaps *adv* 66
piano *n* 50
pick up *v* 30, 33
pilot *n* 18
pink *adj* 10
plant *v* 74
pleasant *adj* 30, 33
plenty of *n* 6
police officer *n* 22, 61
pool *n* 78
principal *n* 10, 13, 25
problem *n* 58, 61, 66, 74, 77
program *n* 74, 77
promise *v* 78
punish *v* 10

R

reach *v* 46, 49, 74
realize *v* 42, 49
reason *n* 74
recently *adv* 70, 73, 74
relax *v* 66, 69
remain *v* 62, 65, 70
repair *v* 38
rescuer *n* 46, 49
return *v* 58, 62, 65

S

safe *adj* 58
safely *adv* 18, 21
save *v* 18, 21, 34, 37, 65
scare *v* 6, 9
scared *adj* 18, 21, 34
search *v* 2
season *n* 70, 73
serious *adj* 74, 77
seriously *adv* 22, 25, 34, 37
several *adj* 2, 5, 6, 30, 62
share *v* 30, 33, 45
should *v* 66, 69, 73
shoulder *n* 62
since *prep* 58
skate *v* 22
solve *v* 66
speed *v* 22, 25, 81
spread *v* 30, 33
step *n* 6, 78
stereo *n* 30
stomachache *n* 2
study [examine] *v* 6
study [learn] *v* 50
succeed *v* 14, 50
success *n* 18
suitably *adv* 10
surprised *adj* 2, 5, 10, 25

T

take care of *v* 6
temperature *n* 78, 81
throw *v* 30, 33
tourist *n* 22, 65, 73
trash *n* 74
turn down *v* 30

U

unbelievable *adj* 70
underground *adj* 58
uniform *n* 10, 13, 22, 25
university *n* 14, 17, 50, 69, 78

W

warn *v* 10
wave *n* 62
wedding *n* 38, 41
wide *adv* 34, 49
wonder *v* 66, 69

5/11   2   2/08